DISCARDED

The Family Butterfly Book

COLLECTION MANAGEMENT

The Family Butterfly Book

Discover the Joy of Attracting, Raising & Nurturing Butterflies

by Rick Mikula

Foreword by Dr. Orley R. Taylor,
Monarch Watch,
University of Kansas

Storey Publishing

The mission of Storey Publishing is to serve our customers
by publishing practical information that encourages personal independence
in harmony with the environment.

Edited by Deborah Burns and Dale Evva Gelfand
Cover design by Meredith Maker
Cover photographs by Giles Prett, except for back-
  cover photograph of Eastern Tiger Swallowtail by
  Bob Wilson
Text design and production by Carol Jessop; art
  direction by Cynthia McFarland

Photography by Giles Prett/SCI, except as noted below:
  Bob Wilson: Pages viii (Monarchs), 2, 4 (top), 6 (chrysalis),
    14, 16, 17, 18, 19, 20, 21 (bottom), 29, 42, 44 (eggs),
    46, 56, 57, 58, 60, 61, 62, 64, 70, 74, 75 (top), 78, 80,
    81, 90, 92, 95 (top), 100, 102, 103, 119 (top), 125 (top),
    130, 133, 137, anc 146 (top)
  Jeff Fengler: Pages 11 (butterfly and skipper), 21 (top), 22,
    23 (top), 24, 25 (top), 26, 27, 36, 45, 58 (hanging
    caterpillar), 84, 95 (bottom), 96–99, 101, 104–118, 119
    (bottom), 120–124, 126–129, 131–132, 134–136,
    138–143, 146 (bottom), and 154. The editor wishes to
    thank Jeff Fengler for his assistance on this book.
  Barbara Howard: Pages 23 (bottom) and 37
  Erik Callahan/SCI: Pages 32 and 73
  Ron Cherry: Page 4 (left)
  Bill Krebs Photography: Page 10
  Rick Mikula: Pages iii (Gulf Fritillary), 47, 72, and 82
  James K. Adams: Page 112

Illustrations of caterpillars, eggs, and chrysalises
  by David Wysotski, Allure Illustrations
Illustration of garden on page 28 by Alison Kolesar
Range maps by Leslie Noyes
Index by Peggy Holloway

Copyright © 2000 by Rick Mikula

The information in this book is true and complete to the best
of our knowledge. All recommendations are made without guarantee on the part of the author or Storey Publishing. The author and
publisher disclaim any liability in connection with the use of this
information. For additional information please contact Storey
Publishing, 210 MASS MoCA Way, North Adams, MA 01247.

Storey books are available for special premium and
promotional uses and for customized editions. Fcr further information, please call 1-800-793-9396.

Printed in Canada by Transcontinental

10 9 8 7 6 5 4 3

LIBRARY OF CONGRESS CATALOGING-IN-PUBLICATION DATA

Mikula, Rick.
    The family butterfly book. / Rick Mikula.
      p. cm.
      ISBN 1-58017-335-7 — ISBN 1-58017-292-X (pb)
      1. Butterflies as pets. 2. Butterfly gardening. I. Title.

SF459.B87 M55 2000
638'.5789 — dc21   00-041996

DEDICATION

This book was written for Lynn Gliem.

Adventurers have traveled the world over in search of things of priceless beauty. They have quested for the amazing and interesting that would fill their senses with wonderment. They have sought jewels and things thought precious from far-off lands. Often they pursued flying jewels, the butterflies. Just by their mere presence, butterflies have always captured attention and captivated their admirers. Delicate, yet strong beyond belief, they are capable of amazing feats. They have the power to brighten any day and always leave their observer spellbound and with a sense of loss when they depart. They make the world a nicer place whenever they are around. They are truly amazing.

Lynn is the consummate butterfly. She has become my closest friend and most trusted confidante. Together we have celebrated life and cheated death. We have shared tears of laughter and sorrow and boldly sought out new adventures. Whether it was the best or worst of times, she was always there. No matter what the situation, she always meets it as would a butterfly, with grace, style, and undying determination. And in the aftermath, she leaves everyone awed with her resourcefulness and fascinated by both her inner and outer beauty. Always strong yet always enchanting, she is like a butterfly.

Likewise, if a butterfly were ever reincarnated into human form, and were she fortunate enough, she surely would be made in the image of Lynn.

I dedicate this book with love to Lynn, always the ultimate butterfly!

CONTENTS

FOREWORD

Two generations ago, most Americans either lived in the country or were connected to the rural way of life through visits with close relatives. They knew about livestock, crops, bees, insects, wildflowers, and wildlife. They didn't have to explain to their children that milk came from cows and eggs came from chickens; the children could see this for themselves. If chicken was on the menu for Sunday dinner, someone had to catch it on Saturday.

Today most of us are disconnected from the natural world around us. In fact, we are conditioned to avoid contact with living creatures. Entomophobia, or the fear of insects, appears to be increasing. We push nature away with our insecticides, herbicides, and power mowers.

Partly to compensate for the resulting lack of exposure to "nature," city children are taken on field trips to farms, petting zoos, and the "wildscapes" of managed parks. However, this exposure is brief and the number of children who are real naturalists and know the organisms around them seems to be diminishing rapidly.

I teach a course on the biology of honeybees to biology students. When I first started teaching the course, I assumed that biology students would know something about plants and that I could simply mention the plants from which the bees obtain nectar, pollen, and propolis. But the students don't know the plants, even the most common species. For most of them, and I suspect for most people, plants are green and they come in different sizes like trees, shrubs, and weeds. Flowers are something else. A cynical colleague felt that a suitable classification for birds based on most people's knowledge would be "little brown birds, big brown birds, and owls."

Insects, arguably the most diverse group of organisms (more than a million species) with which we share the planet, are generally recognized as cockroaches, mosquitoes and flies, bees and wasps, ants, beetles, and moths. And, these are pests! They are something to get rid of, nothing of interest. Right? No, wrong! Insects are fascinating, and with our busy lives and largely isolated urban existence, they (together with the plants and other resources they use) provide an easy way to reconnect with the natural world around us. Among the most fascinating insects are the butterflies.

The author of this book, Rick Mikula, has given you a gift. He guides you in a manner that will allow your whole family to connect with this marvelous group of organisms. He does this by drawing on his vast personal experience with butterflies and his knowledge of techniques and pitfalls, acquired through mentoring hundreds of people as they've begun learning about butterflies. You will come to appreciate their beauty, complex life cycles, and relationships to other organisms. Improving habitats for butterflies gives gardening another purpose, and you will find that rearing and mating butterflies can be an enjoyable activity for the whole family.

I guarantee that once you become familiar with butterflies, you will regard the plants and the other small creatures around you with greater interest.

Orley R. Taylor, Ph.D.
Director, Monarch Watch
www.MonarchWatch.org

PREFACE AND ACKNOWLEDGMENTS

The destruction of habitat is killing butterflies. The more asphalt we lay, the fewer butterflies we will see. The more wildflowers we replace with hybrids and ornamentals, the fewer caterpillars we will find. The more insecticides we spray, the fewer the wings that will fill the sky. Nine out of ten butterflies never reach adulthood. If the eggs aren't crushed or the caterpillars eaten, the adults will probably die of thirst or drown in pesticide somewhere along the way.

Butterflies desperately need our help! They need healthy surroundings in order to survive. By supplying the proper elements, you can help them beat the odds against an early demise, and this book will help you accomplish that goal.

"We don't take them, we make them," I like to say. There is no need to take butterflies from nature when you can help create them in your yard. This book will give you information on gardening and habitat construction that will allow butterflies to flourish. It will help you nurture them into becoming lively, healthy adults. It will even make you a better person by assisting you in becoming butterfly friendly!

There are some people that I would like to acknowledge. All of them are family in one way or another. Some are members through shared DNA; others, through our shared love for butterflies. In one way or another, they have helped me along the way and become part of my family.

First is my wife, Claudia, who allows me to get away with this lifestyle and doesn't force me to get a real job. She is the person most responsible for my books being written. Next is my big brother Jack. One fateful day, he invited me to lunch to propose we enter an exciting new frontier called the World Wide Web. A short time later, the Butterfly Web site was born. After countless hours of hard work from my niece Pam and nephew Neil, the site developed into the invaluable butterfly resource that it is today.

Unfortunately Neil received his wings early and rose to heaven, but he still smiles down on us reassuringly and guides us spiritually. Thanks Jack! Thanks Pam! Miss you Neil!

Next is my adopted butterfly family. The "First Lady of Butterflies" in the United States is Bethany Homeyer. I consider her my little sister. A day without Bethany is a day without butterflies. There is a gentle mountain many people call Steve Connelley; I call him "brother." I swear we were separated at birth. Next is Dale McClung, who is always busy making discoveries, inventing things, and just having fun. His laugh will take the gray out of any day. Jacob Groth is amazingly knowledgeable and an inspiration to anyone fortunate enough to know him. He is the younger brother that would make any family proud. Cousin Linda Rogers produces more electricity than Hoover Dam. Her contagious energy and marketing savvy can move mountains. Jay and Edie McRoberts and Gary Cousins are the type of friends that everyone should be privileged to have. Kindly Uncle Carmen Panella showed up on my doorstep one morning and taught me how to communicate at a child's level. A more priceless gift I have never received. Amazing Uncle Julian de la Rosa taught me more about the history of North American butterflies than anyone else.

Other individuals that I'd like to thank are Jeff Fengler; Bob Wilson; Robert R. Muller for permission to photograph his butterfly collection; Paula Plock's fifth-grade class at Williamstown (MA) Elementary School; Dr. Wayne Wehling of the USDA for his guidance and desire to help all butterflies; and of course Dr. Chip Taylor for his valuable time writing the foreword for this book. Thanks to all of you.

Rick Mikula
Hole-in-Hand Butterfly Farm
Hazleton, PA

Getting to Know Butterflies

I Didn't Know That!

Have you ever heard that if you touch a butterfly, you'll rub off the powder from its wings, and it will die? Or that if a butterfly gets a drop of water on it, it will drown? Ever hear that a torn or broken butterfly wing will grow back? And everyone knows that all butterflies go to Mexico for the winter, right?

Well, if you believe any of that, I've got a few acres of swampland I'd like to sell you. Because, you see, none of these statements is true. (If you want to know what *is* true, you're going to have to keep reading.) A lot of myths like these were probably started with the best intentions, so that people wouldn't harm butterflies. Many people believe that butterflies are such delicate creatures that they would die in the simplest breeze or anything less than perfect conditions.

The truth is, butterflies have evolved to survive and thrive in extreme conditions. They exist everywhere in the world except for Antarctica. They are more in danger from environmental threats caused by humans than from natural weather conditions. They are hardier than we give them credit for, and they survive despite human intervention.

Butterflies are surprisingly tough little creatures that have evolved to survive in cold and heat, wind, rain, and drought.

The Zebra Longwing is so striking that Bronze Age artists painted its image on cave walls.

TERMS TO KNOW

"Leps" is the cool way to refer to butterflies. It's short for *Lepidoptera*, the Greek word for the order of butterflies, moths, and skippers. (*Lepidos* means "scales," and *ptera* means "wings.") That ancient Greek know-it-all Aristotle coined that term as well as the word **entomology**, which means, of course, the study of insects.

Aristotle's fellow Greeks demonstrated their appreciation of butterflies by coining the word **chrysalis,** which is Greek for "gold." Their beloved deity Psyche had the body of a woman and the wings of a butterfly. Today we relate Psyche's name to dealings of the mind, but to the Greeks her name meant "soul" and "breath," as well as "butterfly."

In Love with Butterflies

It seems that every society loves butterflies, and this goes all the way back to the dawn of civilization. Some butterfly petroglyphs date to the Bronze Age. On a trip to the Dominican Republic, I was privileged to see petroglyphs on the walls of a cave called Cueva de Borbon. The unknown ancient artist had painted the butterflies so accurately that it was easy to recognize the species as a Zebra Longwing.

The first entomology reports ever recorded in the New World were written off the coast of the Dominican Republic, by none other than Christopher Columbus in October, 1492. In his ship's log, Columbus described the large clouds of yellow butterflies that surrounded his vessels as he approached the island.

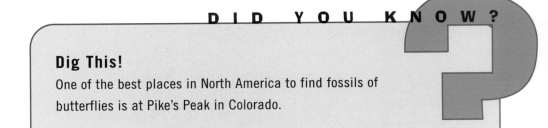

DID YOU KNOW?

Dig This!
One of the best places in North America to find fossils of butterflies is at Pike's Peak in Colorado.

Flying Flowers

Columbus didn't introduce the joy of butterfly watching to the New World, of course. Native Americans apparently always had a fascination with butterflies. The Aztecs believed their god Quetzalcoatl entered the world as a chrysalis, then transformed into a butterfly. The Aztecs also believed that the "happy dead" would come back to visit in the form of a butterfly. Aztec men of high rank often carried great bouquets of flowers for visiting butterfly relatives to enjoy. Mortals themselves were forbidden to smell the flowers from anywhere but the side because the fragrance at the top was reserved for the butterflies.

This belief in reincarnation is still celebrated during the traditional Mexican Day of the Dead festivities on November 1 and 2. Whether coincidentally or not, the holiday nicely corresponds to the time when migrating Monarchs arrive at their overwintering sites. In the small town of Janitzio, fishermen load their "butterfly boats" with offerings of food and flowers that are taken to the cemetery for departed relatives.

Many Native tribes referred to butterflies as "flying flowers" because of their wonderful, often iridescent colors.

The Tiger Swallowtail is one of many butterflies that are native throughout North America, even as far north as Alaska.

Native American Traditions

Farther north from Mexico, the Blackfoot tribe was sure that butterflies brought dreams, and the women would place embroidered butterflies beside their children when they wanted them to go to sleep. And the Flatheads of Montana depicted the metamorphosis of various leps in their pottery, developing their art to such a high level of accuracy and detail that it's quite easy to identify the species being honored.

The Hopi also used butterflies in prehistoric pottery and Kachina figures; Poli Taka was the butterfly man, and Poli Mana was the butterfly girl. The most prominent members of the Hopi people were the Butterfly Clan, who took great pride in their butterfly dance.

The neighboring Zunis called the butterfly man Poli Sio, while the nearby Navajos called him Begochidi. Legend has it that the Great Spirit instructed his human children to whisper wishes to these colorful messengers, who would then carry the wishes to his sky lodge for granting.

This Hopi Kachina figure depicts the spirit of the butterfly, called Pcli Taka, or the Butterfly Man.

DID YOU KNOW?

North to Alaska

Believe it or not, there are more species of butterflies in Alaska (78) than in Hawaii (17). The reason the range of butterflies has expanded northward is that they can travel along a "biological bridge" to Alaska and northern Canada, following their favorite plants along coastline, mountain ranges, and river valleys. To migrate to Hawaii, in contrast, butterflies have a hit-or-miss journey way out into the Pacific Ocean. A few butterflies have made this journey, but many more Hawaiian species have been introduced or brought by accident.

Butterflius Giganticus

The rarest of all butterflies just may have been the Tunguska. It was discovered in Siberia and had a wingspan of 50 miles. In 1908 an asteroid entered the atmosphere and exploded 5 miles above the Tunguska forest. The explosion left a scorched 1,200-square-mile impression on the Siberian countryside in the shape of a giant butterfly.

Modern Lore

Butterfly lore continues to this day. In the Philippines, a black butterfly is a sign of bad luck. A Filipina acquaintance of mine lived, ironically, on Lepdos, the island of butterflies off the coast of Greece. One morning she was surrounded by a group of black butterflies while jogging. Remembering childhood folklore, she became frightened and ran home. As she entered her house, the telephone was ringing. It was her mother calling from the Philippines to tell her that her father had just passed away. Eerie but true.

In the Caribbean nation of Aruba, many people feel that a black butterfly is a messenger of death. Most often, though, the butterfly is a sign of good luck. In the Ozarks, one of the best things that can happen to a new bride is to have a butterfly land on her — definitely a sign of fortunate days ahead.

It is a lucky bride who has butterflies alight on her.

Caterpillar and Butterfly Anatomy

A butterfly goes through developmental phases that are remarkably different from one another. Although each species is unique, here are some general characteristics.

The Caterpillar

The caterpillar's body has thirteen segments. Because its skin doesn't stretch, the creature must shed the skin, or **molt,** several times as it grows. Each stage of growth is called an **instar.**

A Monarch caterpillar is up to 2 inches (50 mm) long.

CATERPILLARS HAVE SIMPLE EYES CALLED OCELLI, AND THEY CAN TELL ONLY WHETHER IT'S DAY OR NIGHT.

THE CATERPILLAR'S POWERFUL JAWS RARELY STOP CHEWING.

THREE PAIRS OF JOINTED TRUE LEGS PLUS SEVERAL PAIRS OF NONJOINTED LEGS MOVE THE CATERPILLAR.

The Chrysalis

The caterpillar's final instar produces the chrysalis. A caterpillar spins silk and creates a chrysalis with the help of **spinnerets** on its mouth. Then, inside the chrysalis, occurs the remarkable transformation known as **metamorphosis.**

The **cremaster** is the projection on the end of the chrysalis that attaches to a stem, twig, or other firm surface.

A Spicebush Swallowtail chrysalis is up to 1¼ inches (30 mm) long.

The Butterfly

Adult butterflies have six legs, though most seem to have only four. In some species, the front legs are so small that they're almost undetectable and are used only for grooming the proboscis. **Tarsi** are the butterfly's equivalent of claws and are used for clinging to a petal or leaf.

A Zebra Longwing butterfly has a wingspan of up to 3¾ inches (80 mm).

THE BUTTERFLY'S LONG PROBOSCIS, MADE UP OF TWO PARALLEL TUBES, UNCOILS TO SUCK NECTAR AND OTHER LIQUIDS.

UNLIKE THE CATERPILLAR'S EYES, WHICH ARE SIMPLE, THE BUTTERFLY'S COMPOUND EYES CAN SEE ULTRAVIOLET LIGHT. IN FACT, BUTTERFLIES HAVE MARVELOUS EYES THAT CAN SEE IN MANY DIRECTIONS AT ONCE, AND IT'S THESE COMPLEX FACETS THAT ALLOW BUTTERFLIES TO DETECT MOVEMENTS BY THEIR PREDATORS.

A BUTTERFLY'S ANTENNAE ARE USED FOR BOTH TOUCH AND SMELL.

THE WINGS ARE TRACED BY VEINS THAT PROVIDE STRUCTURE AND TRANSMIT FLUIDS.

THE ADULT BUTTERFLY'S BODY CONSISTS OF THE HEAD, THORAX, AND ABDOMEN.

BUTTERFLIES HAVE FOUR WINGS, TWO FOREWINGS AND TWO HIND WINGS, WHICH CAN WORK INDEPENDENTLY OF EACH OTHER.

A BUTTERFLY'S FEET CONTAIN TASTE ORGANS. WHEN THEY TOUCH NECTAR, THEY PROMPT THE PROBOSCIS TO AUTOMATICALLY UNCOIL.

A BUTTERFLY'S ENTIRE BODY IS COVERED WITH MODIFIED HAIRS CALLED SCALES, WHICH ARE MOST NOTICEABLE AS A POWDER THAT COVERS THE WINGS. THE COLORED PATTERNS THAT THEY FORM HELP THE BUTTERFLY FOOL PREDATORS, FIND A MATE, AND GATHER HEAT SO THAT IT CAN FLY.

Water on the Wings and Other Common Myths Debunked

Does a drop of water damage a butterfly's wing? Well, in fact, I've often noticed butterflies enjoying leisurely flights through midsummer rains. I've even occasionally found them floating in the watering dish of my atrium, seemingly having met with an early demise. But whether they were bent on suicide or just slipped in the tub while taking a bath, once fished out and placed in the sunlight, they quickly dried out and flew away.

Is it true that rubbing the powder off the wings will make a butterfly unable to fly? No. The powder on a butterfly's wing is composed of thousands of dust-sized, loosely attached scales, which are shed throughout a butterfly's life. These modified hairs, which are positioned like shingles on a roof, have a number of functions. They help retain body heat. They streamline airflow for easier flight. The fact that they are shed easily may help the insect escape from sticky spider webs. The color patterns formed by the scales are particularly important not only for locating the proper mate but, in many instances, for camouflage. Without any scales a butterfly could still fly, but it would lack the advantages of color for courtship and protection.

Can torn or broken wings regenerate themselves? No. Once a butterfly's wing is damaged it can never repair itself. Unlike certain reptiles that can rebuild their tails, leps cannot rejuvenate new body parts. A torn wing can be repaired to a certain extent with tape or glue but, if left to Mother Nature, it will only deteriorate quickly.

How to Handle a Butterfly

Before handling a butterfly be sure that your hands are dry. With your thumb and index finger, grasp the butterfly by the wings just above the body and as close to the butterfly's shoulders as possible. This will reduce extra flapping and eliminate damage to the wings. Very light pressure is needed, and it is a quickly acquired skill. In this fashion it is possible to handle the same butterfly many times with minimal scale loss.

If the butterfly seems agitated, turn it upside down. This will immediately calm it.

Name That Lep

Early European settlers so appreciated the resident American leps (though they unfortunately showed their appreciation by collecting them by the thousands and sending them back to Europe) that they developed many of the butterfly names we know today. For example, the Lord Baltimore, now referred to as the Baltimore Checkerspot *(Euphydryas phaeton),* was named for 17th-century colonist George Calvert, the first Lord Baltimore, because the butterfly's colors matched those on his heraldic shield. And in fact it was the Pilgrims who named the Monarch; they believed that the golden stripe encircling the top of the hanging chrysalis resembled the golden crown worn by their own monarch, King James I of England.

Monarchs are the most familiar of North American butterflies and range over most of the continent.

TERMS TO KNOW

The most accepted theory of how butterflies received their name goes back to the British Isles. One of the more common species there was the Yellow Brimstone. Apparently, people first referred to it as a "butter-colored fly." It wasn't long before the word was shortened to "butterfly."

This tree, laden with overwintering Monarchs, was photographed during the peak of the migration in Michoacan, Mexico.

Going to Extremes

The largest of all leps is the Queen Alexandra Birdwing of Papua New Guinea, with a wingspan of 12 inches. The smallest butterfly of all, the Pigmy Blue, is found in Texas, where everything is supposed to be bigger. It has a wingspan of only ¼ inch.

Long-Distance Travelers

Whatever size their wings may be, many leps are capable of great flights. The Painted Lady of Europe will make seasonal flights to Africa. And Cloudless Sulphurs, which normally inhabit the Gulf Coast, can often be found as far north as New York state as a result of natural fall dispersal.

In North America (unless, as happens occasionally during fall migration, they're blown off course and find themselves on the English coast) Monarchs regularly migrate from Canada to Mexico and return the following summer. Or at least their progeny do. No individual Monarch actually completes the round-trip migration. After wintering in Mexico or California (depending on where they start out), the butterflies head north and breed along the way. It's their offspring that return to the starting point. Researchers have no clue how butterflies navigate this astonishing journey.

All this traveling seems like an awful lot of work, considering that most butterflies are adults for only two weeks, though a few do survive for a few months. The longevity champion is not a butterfly but rather a larva, the tiny Banana Yucca Moth caterpillar, which is able to wait 30 years to form a pupa, or chrysalis, and then finally emerge in its adult form.

Skippers

Whereas the Monarch is our most recognizable and familiar North American butterfly, the least familiar leps are the skippers, which aren't actually true butterflies (Papilionidae) but rather belong to the family Hesperiidae. The novice may easily confuse these generally unimpressive leps with moths. Skippers aren't very big; they're certainly not colorful — at best one subfamily manages a tawny orange, while the other subfamily is brown, gray, or black. And, being rather squat and hairy, they're far from what most people would consider pretty. But there are about 3,000 species worldwide, and they can fly in short bursts of 30 miles per hour, about the speed of a cruising cheetah. Their name was inspired by their flight pattern, which resembles a stone skipping across the surface of the water. While they look like hybrids of butterflies and moths, skippers can usually be identified by their antennae (see photo below).

But even skippers seem like slowpokes compared to their largest-winged cousins, which can achieve a burst of 45 to 50 miles per hour.

Antenna Differences among Butterflies, Skippers, and Moths

Butterflies, skippers, and moths can be readily distinguished by their antennae. The antennae are used for both smelling odors and feeling things.

Butterfly antennae are straight and thin and end as a bulb or ball. This is a Great Spangled Fritillary.

Moth antennae are shaped like little feathers. This is a Cynthia moth.

Skippers have straight antennae that curve back at the tip like a fishhook. This is a Silver-Spotted Skipper.

Butterflies in Danger

Ah, butterflies . . . colorful and gentle and floating through their day as we all wish we could. Our love affair with leps has never been more evident than it is today, given the specialized gardens being grown, magazines being published, and clubs being organized just to help these little critters. It seems that life couldn't be any sweeter for them, right? Unfortunately, that is just not so.

Urban Sprawl vs. Caterpillar Crawl

Butterfly species are disappearing faster than ever before. The more wild-flower meadows that are dug up and replanted with shopping malls, the fewer butterflies we will see. Urban sprawl will eventually eliminate caterpillar crawl. Yes, butterflies are adaptable, but they can't possibly compete with us. We can now travel to any place in the world we want to in record time, but the roads and airport runways that take us there have covered over butterfly habitats. Some wonderful meadow that seems like the perfect place to construct a home was probably a nursery to thousands of little leps every summer for hundreds of years. And now there's a new threat: food crops that are genetically engineered to produce their own insecticides. Unfortunately, insecticides kill insects (that's their job, and they do it well) and butterflies are, after all, insects.

Fair-Weather Friends

Butterflies can't fly if the temperature is below 60°F. Their body fluid, **hemolymph,** becomes too thick and restricts the flight muscles from working properly. At that point, they would much rather take a nap.

D I D   Y O U   K N O W ?

From Tropics to Tundra

It's estimated that nearly 17,000 species of butterflies can be found worldwide; about 780 live in the United States and Canada, along with 11,000 species of moths that have been recorded. And new species are being discovered regularly. But the U.S. Fish and Wildlife Service lists around 20 butterflies and moths as endangered or threatened. Most of these species may well become extinct due to loss of habitat. This is the biggest problem facing all butterflies.

Among the most threatened are the Schaus Swallowtails of Florida. At one time they numbered less than 100. Fortunately, through dedicated efforts of butterfly devotees, they are now making a comeback.

A water source and a variety of blooms will attract butterflies throughout the growing season.

Creating a Butterfly Habitat

"Progress" is inevitable, of course. *Homo sapiens* is a significant species on our planet, but humankind's actions are causing our fellow inhabitants to suffer and in many cases perish, often to the point of extinction. We have "technology" on our side. We are winning the battle to expand our living areas at the expense of theirs. That is why butterflies desperately need our help. They need us to use our technology to help them maintain their fingertip hold on the cliff of survival.

The place to start helping is in your own backyard. There needs to be a biological bridge of gardens to attract butterflies from the woodland into the suburban/urban setting. If every neighborhood had one or two butterfly gardens planted, eventually there would be more butterflies for everyone living there to enjoy. It would give butterflies a reason to venture into that city or town. They need color and fragrance, flowers, ponds, trees, even mud, not the cold glare of glass and concrete, the pungent odor of pollutants, or the threat of death on the windshields and grilles of speeding vehicles.

Whether you live in a rural or urban setting, you can do many things to help butterflies beat the odds. Simply turn the page and start to become butterfly friendly. Follow these recommendations, and as time progresses, you'll begin to see more butterflies in your neighborhood. You'll also find suggestions for creating a butterfly-friendly habitat in your own yard.

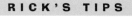

RICK'S TIPS

It's easy to keep your backyard butterflies healthy and happy:

- Use no pesticides

- Create a brush pile in a corner of your property where they can overwinter

- Supply water or a damp place

- Provide a variety of plants that bloom throughout the growing season

Inviting Butterflies into Your Garden

Persuading Butterflies to Come Hither Rather Than Yonder

So you've decided to invite the Admiral and his Painted Lady friend to your garden for afternoon tea. Well, you'd better have the proper refreshments, or they'll leave your garden party for your neighbor's.

If butterflies seem to be everywhere but in your garden, it's time to devise a plan. The correct plants and trimmings can turn your garden into a banquet for your wandering travelers. One lone petunia won't do the trick. Your salad bar will need to be regionalized and specialized because your guest card will be filled only if the proper menu is offered. And with a little tweaking here and there, you can decide just which guests will be coming for dinner.

Garden flowers, such as cosmos, will attract many nectaring butterflies, including the beautiful American Painted Lady.

Facets of Your Garden

You have a multitude of choices regarding variety of plants, maintenance level, and garden size. Generally, your winged friends will greatly appreciate whatever appropriate floral offering you provide, whether large or small. Many people choose all perennials, figuring they're the easiest to care for. Once they're in, they're in, and being perennials, they'll come back every year. Annuals, on the other hand, are exactly that: annuals. Which means they need to be replaced every year.

The Cloudless Sulphur and other small butterflies prefer to nectar from plants with clusters of tiny blooms.

A primary consideration in choosing your plantings, of course, is that certain flowers are more attractive to some butterfly species than they are to others. Much of this preference has to do with the actual structure of the flower. Those with tight clusters of bloom, such as alyssums, are more attractive to small butterflies. Usually, the smaller the butterfly, the smaller its proboscis (drinking tube). Having a smaller proboscis means it's easier to swing around while searching the flower clusters for nectar. Whites, Sulphurs, and Skippers are drawn to such an arrangement. The tiny Metalmarks and Checkerspots also favor the easy-to-reach blooms. Swallowtails, on the other hand, have much longer drinking tubes and find deep-throated flowers more to their liking. Daylilies and trumpet vines are fine examples of blooms that pander to those long-nosed critters.

Only a few aspects need to be addressed for a good old-fashioned butterfly-producing garden, but all of them are crucial to its success.

Region

Don't plant passionflowers in North Dakota in the hope of attracting Zebra Longwings; it's not going to work. Instead, investigate which butterflies live in your region and which plants they find most attractive, and plant those. By addressing your indigenous populations, your success will be much greater.

Feeling the Blues

Little Blues are generally overlooked. Quite lovely, some with very intricate patterns on their wings and others with wonderful little tails protruding from the hind wings, they are fragile leps, and their habitats are the easiest to destroy. Many species live in extremely small areas, some as small as a baseball field, that are probably wiped out more easily than others.

Most Blues thrive on lupines and depend on them for their caterpillars. So plant lots of lupines. Then the Blues won't need to sing the blues.

Seasonality

If all your flowers bloom in June, what's going to lure anything to your garden in August? Butterflies need to be attracted both visually and aromatically, so if all your blooms are spent, there's no reason to visit. Choose a selection of plants that will offer flowers at different times throughout the butterfly's season. And that season extends into September and October. These are often-neglected yet excellent butterfly months, a time when leps are desperately searching for any nectar source that may be available as they prepare for the winter.

Diversity

It's simple reasoning: A larger choice of flowers will have a wider appeal to a greater selection of butterflies. Masses and clumps of certain blossoms are excellent, but a mixed offering is even better. Of course, when purchasing plants, make sure your garden site will afford the plants their required lighting. Do they need full or partial sun? Will they be happier in the shade? A full-sun garden will naturally be the most productive as far as numbers of blossoms goes, but not everyone's yard can provide such a situation. Also, summers seem to be getting hotter, and droughts are becoming more commonplace. So if you live in an area that's prone to drought, you'd be better off choosing drought-tolerant plants.

Match suitable butterfly-attracting flowers to your location. No matter how tempting a certain plant may be, there's no point trying to grow, say, a sunflower in the shade. Don't worry. There's something suitable for every location or situation. With some asking and a bit of reading, you'll have no trouble finding a selection that will work best for you.

The Tailed Blue has tiny tails that are thought to attract predators to the wrong side of its body.

Blending Nectar and Host Plants

If you rely solely on nectar plants to attract leps, you'll get a showing of winged visitors, but they won't stay long. To keep them around to reproduce, not just eat and run, your garden should be a blend of nectar-producing plants and host plants. Here's the difference:

- Nectar plants offer butterflies life-sustaining food.
- Host plants provide places where females can deposit their eggs as well as food for the larval caterpillars to eat.

Old-fashioned plants, such as bee balm (*Monarda* spp.), are attractive to many types of butterfly, such as this Tiger Swallowtail.

Nectar Plants

When you are choosing nectar plants, the standard and older versions work the best. Why? Well, big simple flower heads have easy-to-access and abundant nectaries. In contrast, many modern hybrids and cultivars have had the nectar bred out of them. They may look great and satisfy your aesthetics, but they're actually useless to a butterfly.

If you're starting your butterfly-garden plants from seed from your local gardening centers, check the seed packets. Many are marked as being good for attracting butterflies and hummingbirds. When buying established plants from nurseries, usually signage will indicate which plants are butterfly friendly. (When in doubt, ask!) The choice is fairly wide, and you'll have plenty of colors to choose from that will appeal to you as well as your butterflies. But they won't make a complete garden in and of themselves. For that, you'll also need host plants.

DID YOU KNOW?

Check Out All the Colors
Butterflies have definite favorites when it comes to color. Purple and yellow are the preferred flower colors, followed by white and blue, and then red. The ideal garden should incorporate the colors that butterflies like best.

TERMS TO KNOW

Frass is the term for caterpillar droppings. One way to find caterpillars is to look for frass collecting on the host plant where the leaves meet the stem. A caterpillar is likely to be located just above.

Host Plants

It isn't often that the host is the main course at dinner, but it is true in this case. Host plants are the plants that larval caterpillars eat. They're also the plants that female butterflies lay their eggs on, which is an ongoing enterprise for the females.

Every species of caterpillar has specific types of plants it will consume. Some larvae, such as the Black Swallowtail or Cabbage White, will eat a wide variety of plants. Others consume one type and one type only. Believe it or not, even in the face of starvation, larvae will die if the species-specific host plant is not available.

An interesting point is that some caterpillars may prefer one type of plant in the South but disregard it in the North. Or they may eat it in your garden but not in a friend's only miles away. The reason may be as simple as a variation in the localized pH of the soil. Different soil nutrients will yield different flavors and vitamins in your plants, and such variables might make them less tasteful to your caterpillars. Nothing is etched in stone, and new host plants are discovered constantly, so the suggestions offered here reflect what has seemed to work best in the past.

This Painted Lady caterpillar is devouring a hollyhock leaf.

Plant Smarts

The passionflower is no dummy and can protect itself quite cleverly. The plant produces golden nodules on the stems to confuse the Zebra Longwing. These small orbs fool the female into thinking that the plant is already loaded with eggs, and she will move on. By tricking the would-be mother into not laying her eggs, the plant protects itself from being eaten by the young caterpillars. Believing that there would be too much competition for her babies, the mother-fly searches for a better nursery for the young 'uns.

Favorite Nectar and Host Plants

Plants favored by butterflies run the gamut in color and season and include perennials, annuals, and biennials. Include some of each in your garden to ensure full-season blooming.

For more gardening information, see page 156.

Favorite Perennial Plants for Butterflies

A general list of excellent butterfly perennials for most USDA hardiness zones includes the following, along with their blooming periods:

 = Host plant preferred by caterpillar
 = Nectar plant preferred by butterfly

Asters: late summer to fall

Bee balm (bergamot): summer through fall

Butterfly bush (buddleia): midsummer to fall

Butterfly weed: summer through fall

Clover (white or red): summer to fall

Coreopsis: summer to fall

Dianthus: spring to fall

Lavender: summer

Lupine: late spring to early summer

Mints: all summer

Passionflower: summer to fall

Phlox: summer to fall

Purple coneflower: summer to fall

Sage: summer to fall

Salvia: summer to fall

Scabiosa 'Butterfly Blue': summer through fall

Shasta daisy: summer

Thistle: late spring through fall

Violet: spring

Yarrow: summer

This Zebra Longwing pupa is attached to the tendril of a passionflower.

Favorite Biennial Plants for Butterflies

As is fairly obvious from the name, biennials flower in their second year and in many cases are self-seeding. Though they don't provide the reliability of perennials, they are still worthy of your consideration — they certainly stop butterflies in their flight path when it's time for a drink. The following plants should definitely be considered because of their wide lepidopteran appeal:

Hollyhock: summer

Parsley: green from spring to fall

Queen Anne's lace: late spring through fall

Sweet William: late spring through summer

Favorite Annual Plants for Butterflies

Too many people overlook annuals as if they weren't worthy of a butterfly garden. But after your perennials are installed, fresh-faced annuals can spruce up and add pizzazz to your garden. They allow you the opportunity to change not only the garden's color scheme but its height and visual flow, as well. Annuals take up little space, so use these where you want a splash of color at various times in the growing season:

Alyssum: summer to midfall

Anise: late summer

Candy tuft: spring to summer

Common stock: spring to summer

Cornflower: summer

Cosmos: late summer to fall

Heliotrope: late spring to summer

Impatiens: summer through fall

Lobelia: summer into fall

Marigold: summer into fall

Mexican sunflower: summer to fall

Nasturtium: late summer

Salvia: summer through fall

Scabiosa: summer through fall

Scarlet sage: summer to fall

Verbena: spring to fall

Zinnia: midsummer to fall

The eggs of Sulphur butterflies (magnified here) are spindle-shaped.

The Common Buckeye spreads its striking wings as it nectars.

Beyond Flowers

When planning your butterfly garden, don't limit your choices to flowering plants. Grasses, for example, are not only pleasing to the eye but offer protection to butterflies and seeds to birds. Many attractive ornamental grasses are available, so choose the ones that you like best and that work best in your site. Some varieties can grow quite tall, so consider that factor when choosing. Others may need extra room to spread with age — something many of us can relate to. Most nurseries have numerous varieties on display and will gladly explain the advantages and pitfalls of each. It's their job, so ask questions.

Long-Tailed Skipper eggs are 1 millimeter in diameter, about the size of a period on this page.

Though not usually thought of as essential to a butterfly's well-being, many shrubs and trees are, in fact, host plants to many butterflies and a large population of moths. Shrubs and trees also provide much-needed protection from wind and predators. If you live in a windy site, locate your taller shrubs to provide a windbreak for the garden.

Bushes for Butterflies

When it comes to planting bushes for butterflies, the all-time best choice for butterfly habitat is (what else?) the butterfly bush, or buddleia. Aesthetically pleasing, it's available in many colors. 'Nanho Blue' seems to have the highest sugar content, but with buddleia, you can't really go wrong: To a butterfly, any one of them is a feast. So pick a color that fits your scheme or desire, and the butterflies are sure to go along with your choice.

Some other bushes and shrubs to consider are:

 = Host plant preferred by caterpillar
🦋 = Nectar plant preferred by butterfly

Buttonbush: summer ～

Caryopteris: late summer to fall ～

Crown flower (Calitropis gigantius): summer, or year-round in tropics ～ 🦋

Firebush (Hamelia patens): spring to summer 🦋

Honeysuckle: usually summer to fall 🦋

Lilac: early spring to early summer ～ 🦋

Mimosa (Albizia julibrissin): summer 🦋

Mock orange: late spring to midsummer 🦋

New Jersey tea (Ceanothus americanus): spring to late summer 🦋

Spicebush: midspring ～ 🦋

Trumpet vine: late summer to early fall 🦋

Viburnum: early spring to early summer 🦋

Trees for Butterflies

Trees, too, serve many purposes for butterflies. In fact, many of the swallowtails use them as host plants. Trees can add structure and aesthetic flow to your garden design. Can you center your garden around the existing trees that provide shade and privacy? Will there be just the right spot for a "field station" (a.k.a. a hammock) from which to view the garden during backbreaking hours of scientific butterfly research? (Okay, sure, most people might refer to this enterprise as lying there like a lazy dog, but let's see how well they could lie motionless for hours while butterflies glissade gently past your — ahem — lepidopteran observation post.)

An American Snout egg (magnified here) looks like a tiny dot on a hackberry leaf.

Choose your trees wisely, and ask questions before you buy. Unlike annuals or even perennials, trees will be around for a long, long time and are costly to remove when mature, so think before you plant. For example, don't place willows near water pipes because the roots will entwine them as they search for water. Willows will also drip a messy sap all over your car that is horrible to remove. Many towns also have shade-tree commissions with tons of rules and regulations concerning their plantings.

The following trees are all excellent choices for butterfly habitat:

Aspens	Elms	Oaks
Bottlebrushes	Eucalyptus	Sweet bay
Cherry	Hackberry	Tulip tree
Citrus	Magnolias	Willows

The recommended lepidopteran observation platform.

The Best Regional Backyard Butterfly Plants

I asked friends from around North America which nectar and host plants work best for them in their backyards, and these were their choices, broken down by region. Note that the nectar plants listed are suitable for all butterflies in the region.

Northeastern United States, Southern Ontario, and Quebec

NECTAR PLANTS: Black-eyed Susan, butterfly bush, lilac, New England aster, phlox, purple coneflower, and Queen Anne's lace

HOST PLANTS

RED-SPOTTED PURPLE EGG
(MAGNIFIED) ON BLACK CHERRY

Butterfly	Host Plant
Black Swallowtail	Carrot, dill, fennel, parsley
Buckeye	Snapdragon, verbena
Cabbage White	Nasturtium
Great Spangled Fritillary	Violet
Monarch	Milkweed
Mourning Cloak	Aspen, elm, willow
Pearly Crescentspot	Asters
Red-Spotted Purple	Wild cherry, willow,
Spicebush Swallowtail	Sassafras, spicebush
Tiger Swallowtail	Poplar, wild cherry

The Southeastern States

NECTAR PLANTS: Blue porter weed, butterfly bush, fire bush, groundsel, heliotrope, lantana, and star flower

HOST PLANTS

CLOUDED ORANGE SULPHUR CHRYSALIS

Butterfly	Host Plant
Black Swallowtail	Carrot, dill, fennel, parsley
Buckeye	Snapdragon, verbena
Cloudless Sulphur	Wild senna
Giant Swallowtail	Citrus, wild lime
Gulf Fritillary	Passionflower
Monarch	Milkweed
Pipevine Swallowtail	Pipevine (calico pipe, Dutchman's pipe, rooster flower, Virginia snakeroot)
Polydamas Swallowtail	Pipevine (calico pipe, Dutchman's pipe, rooster flower, Virginia snakeroot)
Red-Spotted Purple	Wild cherry, willow
Tiger Swallowtail	Poplar, wild cherry
Zebra Longwing	Passionflower

The Midwest, Including Manitoba

NECTAR PLANTS: Butterfly weed, cosmos, honeysuckle, Joe-Pye weed, lantana, lilac, Mexican sunflower, New England aster, phlox, 'Silky Gold' milkweed, verbena, and 'White Profusion' butterfly bush

HOST PLANTS

Butterfly	Host Plant
Black Swallowtail	Carrot, dill, fennel, parsley
Great Spangled Fritillary	Violet
Monarch	Milkweed
Pearly Crescentspot	Aster
Pipevine Swallowtail	Pipevine (calico pipe, Dutchman's pipe, rooster flower, Virginia snakeroot)
Red-Spotted Purple	Wild cherry, willow
Spicebush Swallowtail	Sassafras, spicebush
Viceroy	Cherry, plum, poplar, willow

RED-SPOTTED PURPLE ADULT

South Central United States, New Mexico, and Texas

NECTAR PLANTS: Butterfly bush, emperor's candlesticks, Mexican flame vine, passionflower 'Incense', pentas, and tropical milkweed

HOST PLANTS

Butterfly	Host Plant
Cloudless Sulphur	Wild senna
Gulf Fritillary	Passionflower
Hackberry Butterfly	Hackberry
Patch Butterfly	Sunflower
Question Mark	Elm, hackberry, nettle

Because most butterfly eggs are less than 1 millimeter in size, you will need a good magnifying glass to identify them.

The Rockies, Including Southern Alberta, Manitoba, and Saskatchewan

NECTAR PLANTS: Bird's eye, catchfly, coreopsis, globe thistle, purple coneflower, and sweet William

HOST PLANTS

RED ADMIRAL EGG (MAGNIFIED) ON STINGING NETTLE

Butterfly	Host Plant
Great Spangled Fritillary	Violet
Mourning Cloak	Aspen, elm, willow
Painted Lady	Hollyhock, mallow
Pale Swallowtail	Buckthorn, cherry, lilac, wild plum
Striped Hairstreak	Ash, blueberry, wild plum
Weidemeyer's Admiral	Aspen, chokecherry, poplar, willow
Western Tiger Swallowtail	Aspen, cherry, poplar, wild plum, willow

California, Nevada, and Arizona

NECTAR PLANTS: Bloodflower, butterfly bush, lantana, pentas, scabiosa, and strawberry

HOST PLANTS

Butterfly	Host Plant
Anise Swallowtail	Anise, carrot, dill, fennel, parsley
California Dogface	Clover, false indigo, pea
Red Admiral	Hop, nettle
Two-Tailed Swallowtail	Ash, hop tree, wild plum
West Coast Lady	Hollyhock, mallow
Western Tiger Swallowtail	Aspen, cherry, poplar, wild plum, willow

Pacific Northwest and Southern British Columbia

NECTAR PLANTS: Anise hyssop, bee balm, dianthus, phlox, red valerian, and stonecrop

HOST PLANTS

Truly Continental
Monarchs sip nectar from and lay eggs on milkweed throughout North America.

Butterfly	Host Plant
Anise Swallowtail	Anise, carrot, dill, fennel, parsley
Lorquin's Admiral	Aspen, poplar, willow
Meadow Fritillary	Violet
Milbert's Tortoise Shell	Nettle
Mourning Cloak	Aspen, elm, willow
Sara Orange Tip	Mustard
Western Meadow Fritillary	Violet
Zephyr	Currant, elm

Hawaii

NECTAR PLANTS: Balloon plant, bloodflower, crown flower, dianthus, and lantana

HOST PLANTS

Butterfly	Host Plant
Blackburn	Koa
Cabbage White	Cabbage, nasturtium
Citrus Swallowtail	Citrus
Gulf Fritillary	Passionflower
Kamehameha	Mamake
Lantana	Lantana
Monarch	Crown flower *(Calitropis gigantius)*

Alaska

NECTAR PLANTS: Arctic lupine, burnet, California poppy, dame's rocket, Jacob's ladder, goldenrod, Shasta daisy, Siberian aster, wild chamomile, yarrow, and yellow hawkweed

HOST PLANTS

Butterfly	Host Plant
Alaskan Swallowtail	Anise, carrot, dill, fennel, parsley
Arctic Fritillary	Blueberry
Cabbage White	Cabbage
Clodius	Bleeding heart
Mustard White	Mustard
Phoebus	Stonecrop
Silver-Bordered Fritillary	Violets
Tiger Swallowtail	Ash, birch, cherry, poplar
Western Tailed Blue	Pea, vetch

For more gardening information, see page 156.

MEADOW FRITILLARY EGG (MAGNIFIED)

Landscaping for Butterflies

Butterflies have simple needs: food and water and a place to stretch their wings. How these elements are arranged is up to you. And since you're the one putting in all the effort, it stands to reason that you're the one who should find the results most aesthetically pleasing. (Let's face it, the butterflies don't really care which plants are where . . . just that they *are* there.) Think of your garden as your canvas and the flowers as your paints with which to create a masterpiece. Take some time to sit down and daydream about it for a while. Read books on garden and landscape design. Above all, enjoy the process.

Go Organic!

The best fertilizers to use are garden compost and fish emulsions. They are organic and won't poison butterfly larvae.

This easy family butterfly garden will grow almost anywhere in North America.

Landscaping Naturally

Still, some details, such as site placement and plant arrangement, generally work better than others. For example, the ideal location for an effective butterfly garden is a site facing south, or whichever direction will offer maximum sun. However, don't fret if your garden faces west, not south; just go with the flow. Also, keep in mind that when a garden is sited on a slope, shorter-growing flowers look best when placed on the highest part of the slope facing south and along the southwestern edges. The taller-growing selections should be placed along the northwestern edge so as not to take away sunshine from the other flowers.

Of course, if you have a nice flat area, your choices are many. A very lovely effect is a bowl of color created by putting the taller plants around the outside circumference and tapering down the respective heights, ending with the smallest flower circling the immediate center of the garden. It will end up looking like a bowl of flowers. Add a small pond or fountain in the center, and you'll have a striking display.

As for plant placement, setting the tallest plants in the back of the landscape and the shortest toward the front will also create a nice effect. It will broadcast your garden to a great distance since it will be more visible. Only a few flowers of the same height can be seen from up close or directly above, so by tilting your floral palate you'll enjoy more success. Try to picture the garden's flow and its visual impression. Descending flower heights draw the eyes to a focal point or centerpiece, leading the viewer's gaze to where you want it to focus.

Your winged visitors will appreciate groups of the same variety of plant rather than just one of a kind. Groupings offer easy-to-reach nectar all on the same level, so little energy is wasted. Plus, getting from one plant to the other is simple because of the "blanket" effect.

But "all-of-a-sudden clumps" of higher plants amid smaller ones not only create basking sites and perches for would-be lep lovers, they also hide flaws nicely. Say you have a big pipe sticking up in your yard. You can just surround it with some purple coneflowers. Just be creative and do some preplanning. You may be surprised at how beautifully it all turns out.

The spectacular Baltimore Checkerspot will sip nectar from cosmos.

Container Gardening

So you live in the city, which means you don't have a place to create a butterfly garden. Right? Wrong! Container gardens and window boxes work just fine as butterfly lures without taking up a great deal of space. Visit any gardening center, and you'll see that the selection of containers available is truly amazing. There are so many types of materials and styles to choose from that growing in containers is fun to do, even if you have acres and acres to play with. And, no, you don't even need a city-sized garden or a penthouse roof. Containers and hanging baskets also do well on stoops, fire escapes, or landings. And if you live in the 'burbs or out in the country where you do have a full-fledged garden, arranging a few extra oases around your deck or porch will only enhance your habitat.

The absolute best butterfly nectar sources for hanging baskets or pots are 'Star Cluster' or 'Star Flower' *(Pentas lanceolota)* and lantana *(Lantana camara).*

This container garden attracts butterflies throughout the growing season.

RICK'S TIPS

Blooming Beauties

You and your leps can all enjoy year-round pleasure from lantanas and pentas. Kept above 55°F (13°C), they'll stay in bloom continually, so if you live in a cooler climate, bring them into the house and enjoy them all winter . . . if you can provide them with enough light. We keep a resident population of butterflies in our home during the winter months, and they love to nectar from these beautiful, colorful plants.

Designing Container Gardens

When constructing the container garden, place the tallest-growing plants in the center. Surround these with mid-height plants, and finally place the lower-growing edge and trailing plants around the rim of the container. If this mini- garden is to be positioned against a wall or other structure, of course place your flowers accordingly, with the tallest flowers in the back, midrange in the center, and the underachievers — the lowest plants — in the front. This will give you a nice wall of flowers to position against an upright surface.

Morning glories always do especially well in containers and window boxes. Unfortunately they have earned their name justly because they don't stay open all day long. If a bush variety, such as *Convolvulus tricolor,* fits your situation, this is the best choice, since it will stay open all day long and offer more nectaring time for your resident leps.

Plant zinnias and morning glories to attract Monarchs to your garden from midsummer into fall.

Container Plants for Full Sun

Tall	Medium Height	Edge
Aster	Dahlia	Alyssum
Globe Thistle	Marigold	Baby's breath
Heliotrope	Nicotiana	Pincushion
Hibiscus	Snapdragon	Portulaca
Lantana	Stonecrop	Strawflower
Lavender	Thrift	
Pentas	Verbena	
	Zinnia	

Herbs in Containers

Most herbs do well in containers, and when they are in bloom they are irresistible to butterflies. They're easy to care for and do well in a city window box or on a country deck. Anise, parsley, dill, and fennel are particular magnets for egg-laying Anise Swallowtail and Black Swallowtail females. In fact, so are most herbs, including rue, marjoram, mallows, and hyssop, so herbs should always be incorporated into your container or garden plan. Oregano, basil, and lavender make wonderful natural feeders inside my personal butterfly house.

Since most butterflies are solar powered, you'll naturally have more success with a sunnier location. But if your container won't receive full sun during the day or gets only indirect lighting, add flowers like impatiens, caladium, tuberous begonia, lobelia (upright or trailing), polka dot, or flowering vinca.

Winter Survival Strategies

Butterflies living in less-than-tropical areas spend the winters in various forms of development. Depending on their species, they may wait out the colder months as eggs, caterpillars, chrysalises, or adult butterflies, hiding under loose bark on trees, fallen logs, or even the eaves of your house. Frequently, they will adopt an evergreen tree or a pile of firewood as "housing."

A Shady Situation

If your property happens to be in a shady, wooded location, don't fret that you won't get your share of butterflies. In fact, you'll be privileged to see species that sun-drenched folk would never have the chance to enjoy. Spicebush and Tiger Swallowtails love to cruise wooded paths, preferring a rustic setting to a manicured garden. Anglewings, Fritillaries, Tortoise Shells, and Admirals would actually rather dine on fallen fermented fruit than a petunia, and they consider a pile of manure a real epicurean delight.

While the choice of shade-blooming flowers is limited, other things will make your woodsy habitat attractive to butterflies. Most important, maintain fallen logs or loose bark on trees. They are the perfect hideouts for butterflies to pass the winter months in. With a foot of snow on the ground and zero degrees in the air, you could still find butterflies nestled inside waiting for spring.

Most butterflies spend the winter months in various forms, depending on the species. Some spend it as an egg or caterpillar, while others choose the chrysalis or adult stages. Some are exposed to the elements, but most like to find a sanctuary away from hungry predators like mice and birds. A few use leaf litter, but more prefer the camouflage offered by trees and logs. That is why most species that hibernate in the adult stage have cryptic patterns on their wings, which allow them to blend nicely into background bark. This holds true for the other stages of winter nappers.

Look for Spicebush and Tiger Swallowtail butterflies along wooded paths.

Pile It On

Woodpiles are excellent hideaways for overwintering guests, as are fallen logs. Stone walls and even piles of rocks also offer protection to resting butterflies. The first rule: Don't go crazy trying to spruce things up too much for the butterflies. You may well be removing what they're actually looking for. Leave fallen logs in place if they aren't a nuisance and easily tripped over, because they make a safe harbor, as do standing hollow trees (snags). This brings us to rule number two: Use caution before consigning a log to your woodstove or fireplace flames, and always examine stone walls or rocks for stowaways before rearranging them.

An ordinary woodpile is a favorite site for overwintering butterflies. Butterflies in all phases of development may be found between logs.

RICK'S TIPS

Motel Sticks

If you have a stack of firewood on your property, check every log before pitching it into your fireplace or woodstove. These woodpiles offer a safe haven for chrysalises and overwintering adults; in fact, many pupae look surprisingly like a knot of wood and can be easily overlooked. *Help save innocent lives!*

Water

Water is essential to a butterfly, and any way it can be offered is good. Ponds, fountains, misters, or birdbaths will supply what rain and morning dew cannot.

Birdbaths

Birdbaths work better without the pedestal. Many birdbath saucers have decorative patterns and designs on them, and when they're placed directly on the ground, they make a lovely addition to any garden.

Placing a few stones in the saucer to project slightly above the water surface or floating a small piece of wood in the water will make your water feature even more appealing to butterflies. These platforms are perfect resting places and allow your garden guests easy access to the water.

The Lure of Moving Water

If you have a choice of water source, go with moving water. Burbling fountains and waterfalls are good choices, as is a sprinkler, for that matter. Butterflies sometimes float through the mist of a waterfall or garden sprinkler. They seem to enjoy taking showers and can be seen swaying through light summer rains.

Of course, the other advantage of moving water is the calming effect it has on people. Close your eyes and imagine sitting in a warm, colorful garden filled with blooming flowers as you listen to the trickling sound of water in the background. Just then a Giant Swallowtail gently alights on the heavily scented hibiscus directly in front of you. Okay, now open your eyes and get started; the garden center opens at 9 A.M.

A terra cotta butterfly bath like this one will heat up in the sun and provide a drinking source and warm resting place for your visitors.

Build a Waterless Pond

MATERIALS & EQUIPMENT

- Trowel
- String
- Large heavy-duty plastic garbage bag
- Scissors
- Small stones or river rocks (about a wheelbarrowful)

What in the world, you may be asking yourself, is a "waterless pond"? Sounds like a major contradiction in terms, doesn't it? Well, you're right. Mostly. But the beauty of a waterless pond is that it can easily be fashioned in any garden. It doesn't (as the term implies) even require water, yet it will be aesthetically pleasing to you and useful to your visiting butterflies.

On mornings of heavy condensation, it won't require any filling with water. (During the hottest part of summer you may need to add water in the morning with a watering can.) The dew will collect on the rocks and slide down between the cracks. Butterflies can land on the stones and sip the moisture from between them. The heat of the day will evaporate the remaining dew by the end of the afternoon, and you won't have to worry about any buildup of algae. If you choose colorful or interesting stones, your waterless pond may just become the conversation piece of your garden. The dimensions are up to you: There is no set size that will work better than another. Whatever fits into your gardening scheme is the right size and will be appreciated by the butterflies.

1. Dig a hole. Outline it first with string in the shape of a butterfly if you wish.

2. Line the hole with the large plastic garbage bag. It should come to just below the top of the hole. Trim off any excess.

3. Fill the hole with a layer of small stones and river rocks until they are flush with the surrounding area.

Basking Sites

Butterflies are solar powered and need to heat up before they can move or fly. In fact, they can't fly if the temperature is below 60°F or until their flight muscles achieve 83°F. They warm up by shivering or basking in the sunlight. A basking area is therefore an important element in a proper butterfly garden.

A basking area can be as simple as a few light-colored stones or even a concrete walkway. Light colors reflect the sun, and this will heat up the under and upper surfaces of a butterfly's wings simultaneously. The stones of your waterless pond will work for this purpose, and you'll have accomplished two jobs in one. Patio block and stepping stones have come a long way in recent years, and some are very decorative. They'll also work just fine as basking sites, and they offer the additional advantages of being mobile and colorful.

Another option is to create a small band of sand around your water-filled pond. Beach sand works best if you have access to it, and it's saturated with sea salt, which male butterflies love. You may at one time or another have happened on a group of butterflies sipping from a patch of dirt. These are unmated males gathering to imbibe the salts and minerals in the soil, which energize them in preparation for mating. So an offering of salty sand is a good addition to your butterfly habitat.

If a road trip to the beach isn't practical, then visit the local farm and feed supply store for a mineral or salt block commonly used for livestock (these should cost only a dollar or two) and place it in the middle of your sandy area or basking site. Nature will do the rest. Every morning, dew or summer rain will dissolve a little bit of the salt into the ground, replenishing the lads' favorite concoction.

These male Swallowtails are "puddling," or gathering to sip dissolved nutrients from the soil before mating.

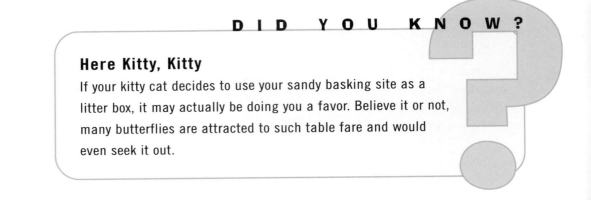

D I D   Y O U   K N O W ?

Here Kitty, Kitty

If your kitty cat decides to use your sandy basking site as a litter box, it may actually be doing you a favor. Believe it or not, many butterflies are attracted to such table fare and would even seek it out.

Ultra Cool

Butterflies see in the ultraviolet range and can enjoy colors and patterns we cannot. So what may not seem attractive to us can drive a butterfly crazy.

Butterfly Condos and Other Lep Lures

Humans are reluctant to accept one simple fact: What nature comes up with to attract butterflies will always be superior to what can be artificially devised. So we keep concocting new . . . well, inventions.

Several years ago the infamous "butterfly house" was introduced to the public. Meant to be a surrogate hibernating refuge, it was thought that it would work like a birdhouse. And look how successful *they* are.

Well, it just isn't so, and butterflies don't like them. It doesn't matter what you place inside to try to attract them because butterflies won't use them. The inventor didn't take into consideration that leps did just fine where they were and weren't house hunting. I know this from firsthand experience. I maintained a few dozen butterfly boxes for several years, and the only residents were spiders and wasps.

Decoys

If you're still in the market for bells and whistles, try a butterfly decoy. Most are made from thin metal and have some sort of patina or coppery finish. The theory here is that reflected ultraviolet rays will lure leps that are ready to mate.

Many species are attracted to or repelled from other butterflies by the ultraviolet colors they reflect. In some species, one sex casts such a reflection but the other does not. This saves a lot of wasted energy that would be spent chasing unsuitable mates. I have seen these decoys in gardens, but I have yet to see butterflies alighting on them. So the verdict is still out on this one. Still, just like the hibernating boxes, they look great, so buy a couple.

Ultraviolet rays may attract butterflies to metal decoys.

What *does* work is tacky. I'm talkin' plastic pink flamingo tacky. In fact, I'm talkin' plastic pink flamingos. Several years ago I was given a pair of these beauties as a garden gift. Much to my surprise, the Swallowtails really enjoyed them. I have yet to see a Tiger or Spicebush fly by without stopping to try to get nectar from them — they work far better than decoys for tempting inquisitive leps into your garden. They aren't at all expensive, and there's no denying that they add a splash of color to the landscape. Some may work and some may not. It all depends on the material used and how that particular color reflects light. If you do get the hue just right, hey, have a few gallons mixed up, and paint the roof of your house. Instant butterfly heaven.

Make Your Own Butterfly Box

MATERIALS

- Half-gallon (1.6 L) cardboard milk carton
- Paper glue or double-sided tape
- Brown bag
- Twigs
- Binder clip or clothes pin
- Scissors
- Paint or crayons

You can make your own butterfly box for basically nothing, and it will be every bit as effective . . . or ineffective . . . as the storebought version. Think of it as a garden ornament rather than as something useful for your leps. This is a great project for kids or families to do together.

Chances are it will never work — and the first rainstorm will put it out of commission — but constructing this butterfly house gives you a chance to enjoy two of the finer, simpler things in life: coloring and butterflies. If nothing else, you've recycled something and spent some quality family time together.

1. Open the top of the container and thoroughly rinse it out with water.

2. Using paper glue or double-sided tape, cover the outside surface of the carton with a section of a brown grocery bag.

5. Your final step is to paint or draw some flowers on your butterfly box before hanging it up. Yellow and purple really turn a butterfly's head, so they make the best choices. Color it all up and have fun.

3. Place some twigs inside the container through the opening in the top. Pinch the top closed and secure with a binder clip or clothespin.

4. Cut two slits ¼ inch wide by 4 inches long into one of the sides. Try to center the slits between the top and bottom and both edges.

Avoid Hummingbird Food

Do not use hummingbird food for butterflies. It's too thick for them and should be diluted with distilled or bottled water. An eight-percent solution is ideal but you can get away with five to ten percent, as mentioned in detail in chapter 3.

Feeders

If the birds and the bees use artificial feeders, it seems only natural that butterflies should, too. Hummingbird-style feeders have been around for quite a while. Recently they've been modified a bit and resold as butterfly feeders. I've had mild success with them, more so in a captive situation than when they're just hanging in the garden, since flowers have aroma and color cues to romance butterflies away from these imitations. They do look unique and make for conversation, but you'll get more hummers than butterflies.

Go Natural

What will work better than a feeder and is all natural to boot is watermelon: pink, juicy watermelon. In a greenhouse setting it's the easiest way to feed a large number of butterflies at once. Cut a slice and place it on a table, and then score the pink pulp with a knife to make some grooves. The juice will collect in the grooves and make it easier for the butterflies to retrieve. Take your butterflies by the wings and put their feet on the watermelon pulp. Their proboscises will quickly uncurl to drink the liquid.

Any fruit left out will also naturally draw ants, bees, and wasps, so use a bit of caution. And never let the watermelon sit out in the blazing sun, as it will soon go rancid. But try this method. It's a lot of fun to feed butterflies with watermelon.

A slice of watermelon is a favorite butterfly snack, and nutritious, too!

Make Your Own Butterfly Net

MATERIALS

- A 4' (1.25 m) length of heavy gauge (¼" or 5 mm) wire
- A 36" x 36" (1 m x 1 m) length of mosquito netting, old panty hose, or net curtain material
- Needle and thread
- Old broom handle or wooden dowel
- Drill with ½" (10 mm) bit

Once your garden is complete, you'll be enjoying butterflies all summer. Sometimes you may want a closer look at your visitors, and one way to do this is by using a net. You'll also need a net to catch butterflies for identification and to collect a female to produce eggs for you. Nets are available at nature stores and through catalogs, but you can create your own with an old curtain, some wire, a broom handle, and some love.

The bag should be twice as long as the opening is wide. Make the bag out of anything from panty hose to old mosquito netting. Fabric store netting is too flimsy, and bridal veil material will catch on everything and rip too easily, so avoid using them.

The handle can be made from any sturdy wooden dowel or a broom handle. Choose a length that is comfortable for you. Longer and thicker handles will be slower to swing than lighter and shorter ones will. PVC pipe is too flexible for a handle, but aluminum works very well. If using a metal pipe for a handle, place the prongs, or "tangs," into the opening of the pipe and then hammer it shut at the end to hold them in place.

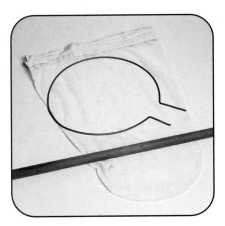

1. Form the wire into a circle, bending a 2-inch (50 mm) perpendicular prong, or "tang," on each end. Sew along one edge of the bag to form a cone shape. Sew a 1-inch-wide (25 mm) hem along the top of the bag.

2. Insert the wire through the hem. Alternatively, you can fasten the bag to the wire with self-sticking carpet edging.

3. Drill a 2-inch-deep (50 mm) hole into the end of the stick. Force the tangs of the metal rim into the hole.

Choosing & Using a Net
When selecting a net, look for a wide mouth and a long handle. The actual bag should be long enough so that when a specimen is caught, the net can be flipped over the opening of the mouth, trapping the butterfly inside. It's all in the flip of the wrist. With a little practice, you'll soon be a pro.

Taking a Butterfly under Your Wing

Oh, Baby!

You've worked hard. The garden is planted, the accoutrements are in place, and you now have butterflies. But in your newly installed oasis you will soon discover new arrivals: the next generation of butterflies, in the form of eggs, caterpillars, and chrysalises. Now what? Are you ready for this responsibility? Don't worry. Not only is it fun and easy to rear butterflies, but it's also the perfect antidote to the worries of our fast-paced human world.

I'll teach you some very simple and inexpensive ways to rear your new charges. You'll add the care and thoughtfulness. Together we'll make the world a nicer and more beautiful place.

The eyespots on the 1½-inch-long (40 mm) Spicebush Swallowtail caterpillar, at left, can fool predators into thinking it's a snake. Above, a paintbrush is the best way to transport a caterpillar, such as this Monarch.

Bringing Up Butterfly Eggs

The age-old question is always: Which came first, the butterfly or the egg? We'll start with the egg.

Laid singly or in groups, butterfly eggs come in a wide assortment of colors, shapes, and sizes. They can be green, purple, ivory, or even silver. They can be round, oval, conical, or squat and flat. It all depends on the species in your area. Keep your butterflies out of direct sunlight at all stages of development.

SPICEBUSH SWALLOWTAIL EGG
(MAGNIFIED)

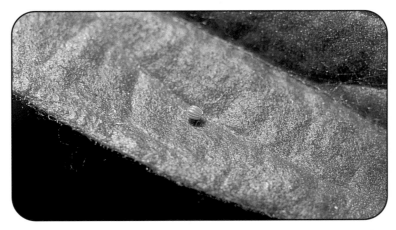

1. Butterfly eggs are usually fastened to the underside of a leaf.

2. Cut the leaf from the stem and place it in an airtight container.

3. On the second day, place a fresh leaf from the host plant on top of the egg.

D I D   Y O U   K N O W ?

What's for Lunch?

A caterpillar's first food is usually its own eggshell. It provides the nutrients the larva will need to begin the next stage of its journey.

Eggs-traordinary!

The best way to find butterfly eggs is to look at the undersides of the leaves in your garden. Once you locate an egg, cut the leaf with the egg attached to it from the stem, and place it in an airtight container, such as a screw-top jar. Don't worry about the larvae suffocating; their need for oxygen is miniscule at this stage.

The container must be airtight to keep the newly hatched caterpillars from escaping. When caterpillars are born, they may be smaller than half an eyelash, so mesh cages, jars with holes in the lids, or hinged delicatessen-type containers, which have tiny openings at the hinges, just won't keep them confined. They will emerge, see the sunlight, and be gone.

Killing butterflies — at any stage — is easy; keeping them alive is the tricky part. Many *ova*, the Latin term for eggs, are thin shelled and will rip easily, killing the embryo inside. So it's very important that you don't remove the egg from the leaf. Just place the egg intact on the leaf into your container.

The next most important thing is *never* to leave the container in direct sunlight, or the creatures will overheat. Also, the newly hatched larvae will be drawn to the sunlight, completely ignoring food. Their instinct to walk toward the light will be so strong that they will actually starve to death. (This insistence on following instincts rather than using intelligence may be one reason why butterflies don't become rocket scientists.)

The eggs will hatch in a few days, but in that time the original transporting leaf will have dried up in the rearing chamber and become useless as food. So, after the second or third day of eggdom, place a new, small piece of the host leaf on top of the egg. This will not only add the humidity needed for emergence, it will also serve as a quick meal. The piece of leaf should be changed every day, so that it will be fresh when the caterpillar decides to hatch.

Hatching

Often you'll notice a hole developing on the surface leaf before you realize that your newly hatched caterpillar, with its amazing appetite, is what caused it. In many cases, though, you'll get a clue about the impending birth because the tip of the egg will turn black directly before it hatches. This black area is actually the developed head of the caterpillar getting ready to munch its way out of its shell and make a break for freedom.

A newly hatched Swallowtail caterpillar is about the size of a comma on this page.

Singular or Plural?

Most often, butterfly eggs will be found alone. The female separates them so that her babies won't be competing with each other for food . . . at least, that's what the experts say. But every now and then you'll find a mother who doesn't have time to read the latest butterfly book, and she'll lay more than one egg per plant, especially when in captivity. What else can she do? She has a short life span and a few hundred eggs to deposit, and she has to go somewhere. So when confined to a small area, as when butterflies are raised by humans, she'll overload a host plant. In the wild, where there are more succulent maternity wards to choose from, she'll distribute the eggs sparsely over a wider area.

Molting is the term for shedding the skin, which a caterpillar must do periodically as it grows, since its skin doesn't stretch. **Instar** is the term for the growing phase that a caterpillar goes through between molts.

The mature Tiger and Western Tiger Swallowtail caterpillars *(Papilio glaucus and Papilio rutulus)* resemble snakes, which helps protect them from being devoured by predators. Their actual eyes are in the first segment of their body.

The Monarch caterpillar grows rapidly between its first (smallest) instar and its last. These photographs show three of the stages at their actual sizes.

Raising Caterpillars

Searching for caterpillars to raise is always a treasure hunt, because they employ ingenious methods to protect themselves from predators, including camouflage. Many are so incredibly well camouflaged that they escape detection even with the closest scrutiny. Some cats are downright ugly, while others are amazingly beautiful.

But just when you think you have mastered the identification game, you're thrown a curve. Many caterpillars go through several color and form changes during the larval period. They may be fuzzy and black for the first instar but white and spiked by the final one. For example, the larvae of Tiger Swallowtails resemble bird droppings when they're small, and when they mature they look like small snakes.

Caterpillar-Spotting Tips

Look for caterpillars on the leaves and stems of wildflowers and garden flowers, and on trees, tall grasses, and the leaves of shrubs. Sometimes you can find a caterpillar by spotting the debris it creates as it munches its way around a plant. Here are some signs:

• Torn and jagged leaves of a favorite host plant
• Clumps of frass (caterpillar droppings) collecting where the leaves meet the stem

First Step: Containment

Let's say you've been successful and you've found a caterpillar. *Now* what do you do? Well, simply remove the entire leaf from the plant and drop it, caterpillar and all, into a waiting container, just as you did with the eggs. One container that has worked well for me is a plastic take-out ice cream sundae dish. Discard the ice cream (it's your preference as to how you do that) and save both halves of the container. Once cleaned out, this will provide a nice, tightly closed rearing chamber for your new charge. Another option is to recycle a margarine tub and soda bottle (see next page).

RICK'S TIPS

Look but Don't Touch
Use a certain amount of caution when dealing with caterpillars. If you aren't completely sure about which caterpillar you've found, don't touch it. Some species can give you a nasty sting or cause a rash. For example, be careful when searching pawpaw trees for Zebra Swallowtails because Saddlebacks, brown caterpillars with green saddles in the center of their backs, can also be found there, and they can cause a stinging reaction in some people. And be leery when examining your shrubs, where you may encounter the hairy Puss moth or Hag moth, both mean- and ugly-looking little stinging caterpillars.

The Zebra Longwing caterpillar is unpalatable to predators because it feeds only on passionflower, which makes it distasteful as well as poisonous. It is not harmful to humans, though.

Make a Caterpillar-Rearing Container

MATERIALS

- Clear 2-liter plastic soft drink bottle
- Scissors
- Small plastic tublike margarine container (of the "I Can't Believe It's Not Butterflies" type)
- Nail or pencil
- Tape
- Scrap of netting or old panty hose
- Strong rubber band

Grow before you throw! Many of the objects that can be used to raise butterflies are probably lying around your house or hiding in the recycling bin.

Here is a great caterpillar incubator fashioned from a soft drink bottle and a margarine container. It costs nothing, and it works. In between residents, just wash out the bottle and let it dry in the sunlight. Once you are finished with it, just toss it into the recycling bin. There now, not only did you save a butterfly's life, but you helped to clean up the earth in the process. Keep the water clean and the plant fresh and you should enjoy many happy butterfly births.

For maximum security, fasten the bottle and the tub together with a strip of tape. It may save hours of tiptoeing around and searching for an escapee.

Note that Swallowtail caterpillars should not be raised in this type of container. See page 81 for more information on their particular needs.

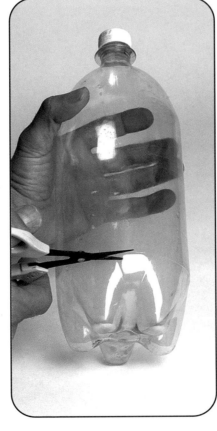

1. Carefully cut the plastic bottle near the bottom where it begins to taper. Follow the seam.

2. Fill the margarine container with water.

3. Poke a hole through the lid with a nail or pencil, and rest the lid on top of the tub.

4. When you find a caterpillar, cut the stem off its host plant and stick the cut end through the hole in the lid. The plant should stand upright in the water.

5. Slide the cut end of the bottle over the top of the host plant and caterpillar, and fit it into the raised lip of the margarine lid.

6. Replace the original plastic bottle top with a scrap piece of panty hose or curtain secured with a rubber band.

Tarsi, the claws on butterfly feet, are useful little features. They help the adult climb up silk paths laid down in the caterpillar phase. Females also use them to scratch plants in their search to find the perfect host to lay eggs on. Remarkably, tarsi also have a sense similar to taste and stimulate the proboscis to uncoil to drink.

Leave fresh host plant material in the bottle until the caterpillar becomes a chrysalis.

Room to Grow

With this easy-to-make setup, when the caterpillar is ready to change into a chrysalis, it will fasten itself to the top or side of the bottle. At that point, remove the plant material. The adult won't need it for food. Again, *never place the container in direct sunlight, or the chrysalis may dehydrate and die.*

There is plenty of space in this larval nursery for a newborn butterfly to dry its wings and stretch its muscles. If by some chance it falls, it should still be able to climb up the sides of the bottle because, as a caterpillar, it coated the inside of the chamber with a network of silk. The adult has tiny hooks on its feet, called *tarsi,* so it can grip the silk and climb back up to let its wings dry. To be on the safe side, put a twig or small branch inside the bottle for the butterfly to climb on.

How to Move a Caterpillar

If you find that you need to separate a number of small larvae, because of either overcrowding or excessive condensation buildup, use a tiny paintbrush, such as a number two sable artist's brush. Place the bristles just underneath the caterpillar's head, perpendicular to its body. Rotate the brush away from the caterpillar, but keep it underneath the head. The bristles will catch the cat's front legs and draw it up onto the brush.

Once the caterpillar is removed from the original surface, place it where you desire — say, on a stem. Then reverse the process, rotating the brush away from the caterpillar. This will cause its back end, hind legs, and then front legs to make contact with the stem, and it will quickly take a firm grip on its new home. You will then have one transported caterpillar that was never touched by human hands.

Always handle your larvae as little as possible since many species are very vulnerable at certain stages, and handling could cause death.

A mobile larval transportation unit.

Build a Hanging Butterfly Cage

MATERIALS

- A piece of netting at least 36" (3 m) long
- Two 10" (25 cm) embroidery hoops
- String

You can make a simple cage that works great for keeping adult butterflies. Best of all, it can be constructed for less than $3. This type of contraption was first used successfully by silk merchants 4,000 years ago, and it's still the best idea going.

You will need two pairs of embroidery hoops, preferably 10 inches in diameter, and some netting (you may already have the needed materials lying about the house). Embroidery hoops consist of an inside and an outside hoop. The outer one has a thumbscrew to tighten it against the inner one. As for the netting, any type can be used (old sheer curtains work well) though the netting of choice is called bridal veil tulle and costs around a dollar per square yard. But use what you have, and be inventive. You can make the cage any size, but a starting length of 36 inches will yield a very workable unit.

Keep in mind: The netting color makes a difference. Lighter netting will induce your adults to breed more quickly, while darker colors will keep them calmer.

This project is most easily done by two people.

This butterfly cage is hanging from a simple frame made of spray-painted plastic PVC pipe.

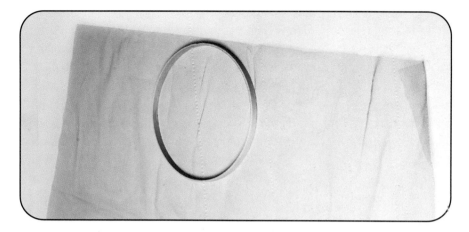

1. Spread the netting horizontally flat on a table and separate the hoops. Then stand one of the inside hoops upright in the center of the material, 10 inches (25 cm) from the edge.

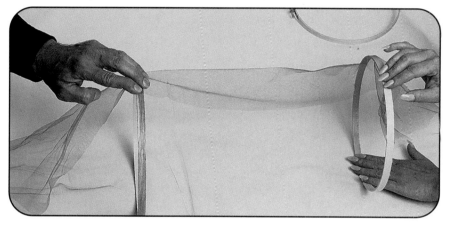

2. Drape one side of the netting over one of the hoops, and hold it in place with your hand. Then bring the other side of the netting up and overlap it by 3 inches (75 mm). This overlap will become the entryway.

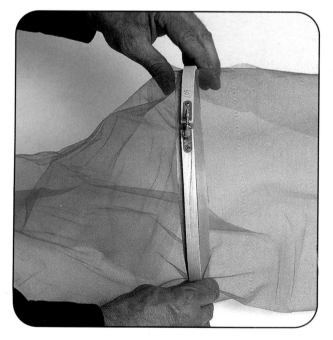

3. Secure the outer hoop over the inner hoop and netting, and tighten the thumbscrew until it's snug. Repeat this procedure with the second pair of hoops.

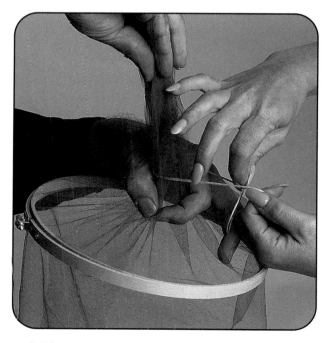

4. When both pairs of hoops are in place, gather the excess material at either end of your newly formed cylinder. Twist lightly and secure with a string that is long enough so that you can tie a loop in it. The loop will be used to hang the entire apparatus.

A Host of Host Plants

Consider growing some of the host plants in small pots, so they can be placed directly inside your hanging cage. Of course, a heavy plant will cause the whole unit to crash to the floor, so hang the cage in such a way that the bottom rests on a tabletop or another supportive surface. The potted plant can then be placed inside, and the female can fill the leaves with eggs.

If you have several pots of host plants available, change the pots after several eggs have been laid. When a plant becomes too loaded, the little mother may stop laying.

Home Sweet Home

With their abode complete, your butterflies can be introduced to their new home. Gently pinching their wings together, slide them through the slit that's formed by the overlapping sides of the netting. Hold your hand in the center of the cage, and release them. They'll quickly cling to the netting.

The soft tulle will not only keep their wings from being injured, it will allow you to give them daily showers. Butterflies love to be misted and groom themselves like cats. During the drier months, you should mist them a few times a day. Every time you spray them, they will instantly extend their proboscises and readily drink the water. To be safe, use bottled or distilled water, just as you would for feeding them.

Chow Time

Speaking of food, it can be served right inside the butterfly condo. If you have a small number of adults, say one to four, you could use a lid from a jar as a serving dish. For a larger number . . . well, this would be the perfect use for those cute little souvenir trays that you may have been collecting.

Whatever dispenser you choose, place some dye- and perfume-free tissue paper into it, and then saturate the paper with an 8-percent sugar-water solution. (If you just didn't excel at chemistry in high school, don't despair. Juicy-Juice and Gatorade make wonderful substitutes, and they are already mixed to just the right proportions. Gatorade also supplies some important electrolytes and trace elements.)

To keep things a bit neater, place a paper plate on the bottom of the cage as a platform to rest the feeding lid on. Then slip the feeding dish through the access slit and stand out of the way of the stampede. It's best to feed butterflies in the morning and remove the tray when they are finished, because the sugar solution may attract ants . . . and ants eat butterflies. (That old food chain can be a tricky thing; that's why it's fun to be at the top.) Your butterflies may well live longer in captivity than they would out in the wild. Once you remove the problem of predators, the odds for a longer life quickly rise.

Small trays make great feeding troughs, and hungry butterflies will gladly feed shoulder to shoulder if the food is good.

Learn to Hand-Feed Butterflies

It's easy to feed butterflies using your own giant homemade cotton swabs.

1. Mix a teaspoon of sugar into a cup of pure bottled or distilled water.

2. Wrap a small ball of cotton around the end of a wooden skewer.

3. Saturate the cotton ball in the sugar-water solution.

4. Place the butterfly on the cotton and watch its proboscis uncoil.

The Mating Game

If you feed your adults in the morning and keep them in ambient light, you should become a proud grandparent quite shortly. Butterflies are particularly sensitive to light and temperature. Any reduction in normal daylight will cause a reduction in activity, including reproductive activity. The same holds true for temperature. Cooler temps will naturally slow them down. (Conversely, if your butterflies get *too* active, move them to an area that has less light or is a few degrees cooler. Basements work well since, being a bit damper than other parts of the house, they give butterflies the higher humidity and cooler temperatures they prefer.)

Great Spangled Fritillaries mate in early summer, but the females don't lay their eggs until late summer. The eggs hatch the following spring, near violets.

The Comma butterfly lays its eggs on hops, nettles, and elms.

The Nuptial Flight
Mating between butterflies often lasts for two or three hours and can occur while the butterflies are airborne.

The Cycle Continues

When a pair is joined back to back by the tips of their abdomens, they are mating. Mating occurs when the male places an envelope of sperm inside the female. At that point, remove any nonmating butterflies and place them in a separate cage. Don't interrupt the mating pair by moving them.

After the mating pair has separated on its own, it's time to put the female to work. The day after mating, the female will begin to alight on plants and taste them with her tarsi. When she finds the proper host plant, she'll deposit an egg onto a leaf. Painted Ladies will lay eggs on anything and everything, especially if that anything is green. And we are talkin' many, *many* eggs on everything. Other species, though, need to have the host plant present to trigger their built-in egg-laying response. As the egg travels through the **ovipositor**, or egg-laying tube, it passes through the sperm sac, where it becomes fertilized. The last thing the female does is to apply a small dab of a gluelike substance to the egg that fastens it to the leaf surface. The egg then develops into a caterpillar . . . and the process starts over again.

To learn how to hand-pair butterflies, see page 77.

The Magical Emergence of a Monarch

When the caterpillar hangs in a J shape, pupation is near.

At first the chrysalis is a satiny green capsule, flecked with gold.

As the butterfly prepares to emerge, the dark wings are visible through the transparent skin.

The butterfly splits the chrysalis and begins to emerge.

The wings are crumpled and damp and must dry before the butterfly can fly.

The butterfly slowly pumps its wings to prepare for flight.

The 2-inch (50 mm) Monarch caterpillar pupates in 10 to 12 days.

Mourning Cloak

EGG

CATERPILLAR

CHRYSALIS

ADULT

Butterfly Life Stages

The eggs, caterpillars, and chrysalises of different species of butterflies are amazingly and intricately different from one another. Here are a few examples.

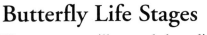

Pipevine Swallowtail

EGG

CATERPILLAR

CHRYSALIS

ADULT

Painted Lady

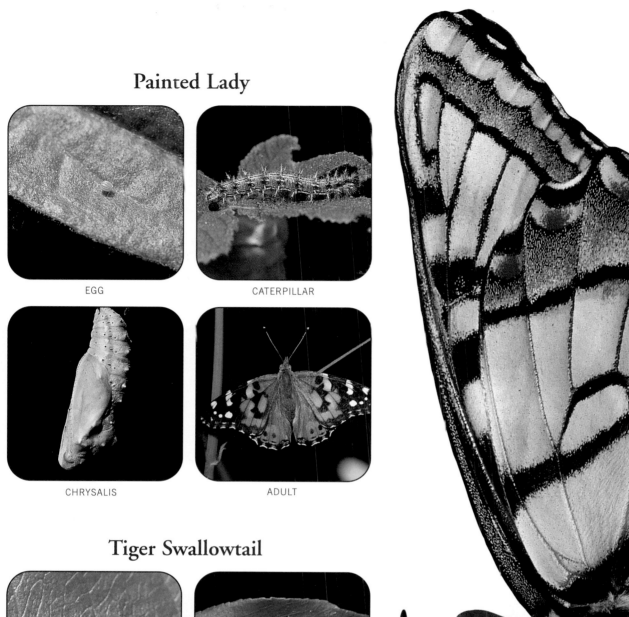

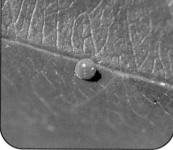

EGG

CATERPILLAR

CHRYSALIS

ADULT

Tiger Swallowtail

EGG

CATERPILLAR

CHRYSALIS

ADULT

EASTERN TIGER
SWALLOWTAIL

To Free or Not to Free

Some folks may consider it cruel to keep butterflies in captivity. But consider that nine out of every ten eggs that are laid in nature never have the opportunity to become adults. They are eaten, are crushed, or die of illness somewhere along the way. If they do make it to the adult stage, they then face a new gauntlet of threats. Birds, insects, speeding vehicles, and pesticides all wait their turn. The two-week life expectancy of most lep adults is usually cut short by any of a number of assailants.

Some butterflies, such as Anglewings and Tortoiseshells, may enjoy adulthood for a few months. Others, such as the nuisance Cabbage Whites, may live for only one week. Whichever species you get to enjoy, do just that: Enjoy it. The few that you nurture won't cause the pyramid to collapse.

If, after all your work, you still feel unsure about keeping your baby, you have a beautiful "out." A Native American legend states that if you want a wish to come true, you must first catch a butterfly, then whisper your wish to it. If you release it unharmed, it will take your wish to the Great Spirit, who will grant it. So once your newborn has hardened its wings and is ready to climb the skies, cup it in your hands, whisper your wish, and set it free.

Most butterflies will stay within a few hundred yards of their birthplace. So whenever you see a butterfly of that species, it just may be one of your grandchildren.

Congratulations!

A class of fifth-graders sends wishes, and butterflies, skyward.

Starting Your Own Butterfly Farm

How Ya Gonna Keep 'Em Down on the Farm after They've Seen *Pieris*?

By this point you've no doubt become so infatuated with the concept of raising butterflies that you're ready to climb into a pair of overalls and get started. Well, the nice thing about raising butterflies is that you can keep your day job or stay in school and still be a butterfly farmer.

Progressing to the next level will require some time and effort, but it'll be well worth it. The advanced techniques in this chapter allow you to rear more of the species you like, plus branch out into a few newer ones for fun. No matter how much of one type you decide to raise over a lifetime, watching a new species emerge is always fascinating.

It's time to get down to some serious farming!

Pipevine Swallowtail caterpillars, which are 2 inches long (50 mm), normally feed on different species of *Aristolochia,* woody vines that make the butterflies unpalatable to predators.

A Breath of Fresh Air

Butterflies and caterpillars don't breathe through their mouths. They use holes in the sides of their abdomens called **spiracles**. These openings are connected to a system of tracheae that deliver oxygen in the same way our lungs do.

Raising a Quantity of Caterpillars

Okay, so now that you have a better understanding of your charges, it's time to get back to nurturing them.

At any level of rearing, it's always best to start your eggs in the airtight incubator containers discussed in chapter 3. These incubators will be used until the hatched caterpillars can be moved into different quarters. How will you know when to move them? That wholly depends on the size of the larvae. Tiny ones are best left in the containers until they can be moved into new quarters for their next stage of growth.

A sign that you have too many caterpillars in one unit will be the formation of water droplets on the inside top surface of the container. Any moisture formation must be avoided because if a droplet falls to the bottom, it will mix with any frass and form a deadly "tea" that may enter the spiracles of the caterpillars (see A Breath of Fresh Air, above) and poison them.

If you see condensation, you'll need to divide the number of caterpillars per incubation container in half. So, say you have ten larvae in a container; remove five, and put them into another container. Keep this up until the cats are large enough that you can put small holes in the top of the container without having to worry about any escapes.

Bottomless Pits

Caterpillars are eating machines. In a two-week period a caterpillar can increase in size by 2,000 times. But compared to some of their relatives, they're shrimps: Some moth larvae will increase in size by 4,000 times.

PAINTED LADY
CATERPILLARS

Containers and Cages

Now here's where the fun really begins. You get to construct your own little kingdom or city — depending on whether you prefer being a monarch (so to speak) or a mayor.

Caterpillar Hi-Rise

Wondering where you'll get so many containers necessary for raising a quantity of caterpillars? Consider using the following inexpensive, practical system. Use hard, clear plastic drinking cups, which easily accommodate a top of netting secured by a rubber band, and put one caterpillar in each cup. This allows your babies plenty of fresh air, and the good ventilation keeps the frass nice and dry for changing time. And plastic cups take up very little space, especially when stacked in the cheap black plastic trays sold in nurseries for bedding plants. (Most nurseries sell their used "nursery pots" for literally pennies apiece.) To maximize use of this small area, go upward.

Figuring one caterpillar per cup, ten cups per tray, and ten layers, you can raise 100 caterpillars using a surface area of just 12 inches by 18 inches. The daily cleaning of "cages" and changing of food are made much easier with this system. Take a few trays to your office or study area so you can watch the caterpillars evolve. (I recommend keeping a spray bottle of water close at hand. Then if anyone should stop in unexpectedly, you can quickly spray your face to simulate sweat — this will garner compassion from friends and loved ones for your obviously vigorous dedication to helping nature.)

TERMS TO KNOW
A **tubercle** is a wartlike bump, often with spines, found along the sides and back of some species of caterpillar.

For maximum efficiency, place ten caterpillar cups on each plant tray. Then lay another tray on top of that one and fill it with ten more cups. Place a third tray on top of the second, and repeat the process until you reach the ceiling.

Good Housekeeping

When your caterpillar cups become dirty, they will need to be cleaned. Remove the caterpillars with a number-two paintbrush as described on page 51. The absolute best cleaner for working with butterflies is a 10-percent bleach mixture. Bleach will kill just about any disease that can kill butterflies. A gallon of solution in a bucket should serve your needs.

Next you need a bottle brush, which can be purchased in a grocery store. They work very nicely in accommodating the odd-shaped sides of your rearing chambers. Dip the cup into the mix, and swish the insides with the brush. Make sure any webbing or silk is removed. Then rinse it with clear water.

The best method for drying the cups is to stack them upside down in a pyramid fashion, with the cups of the upper layer straddling the ones below. This allows better air flow between cups and a quicker drying time. If they can be left in the sunlight to dry, all the better. What the bleach doesn't get, the sunlight will. By using this cleansing system, your cups should serve you for a long time.

RICK'S TIPS

Guano

Frass should never be used for fertilizer. If your caterpillars ever become sick, the disease will be present in the droppings, and if they're used to fertilize your plants, the disease will be passed on to the next generation.

Clean the inside of the cup with a bottle brush, using a 10-percent bleach solution.

A Bucketful of Cats

Many professional breeders use a grander version of the plastic cup: a 5-gallon plastic bucket. Used ones can be found everywhere, for it seems that everything comes in them. The white ones are best, and if they were used for foodstuffs, better yet. At least then you'll know that whatever was inside them shouldn't kill your larvae. Wash the bucket out with a 10-percent bleach solution just to be on the safe side, rinse well, and then wash it out again with soap and water. When you're done, you'll be ready for the big leagues.

For this system, you'll need a piece of netting big enough to overlap the rim of the bucket by 2 to 3 inches all the way around and a length of cord long enough to tie the netting in place. If you can find them, jumbo rubber bands work great.

With this size incubator, an entire stalk of host plant can be put inside. Place the stalk in the bucket upside down. This is especially helpful with sappy plants, such as milkweeds. Most of the sticky liquid will flow back into the stem and leaves rather than puddling on the bottom of the bucket. This lets the plant retain more nutrients, which provides food longer and so reduces your labor. Place the netting over the opening, and secure it below the lip of the rim with the cord. Utilizing the bucket method allows for larger numbers of larvae to be reared with a larger supply of plant material available to them.

The caterpillars will eat their way up the stalk, and, if all goes well, they'll form their chrysalises right on the netting. When a goodly number have done this, the netting is then removed and hung on a wall. The chrysalises will be secured by their own design and will quite happily remain this way until emergence time. The newborns can easily get a foothold on the netting and pull themselves free of their pupal cases. With tarsi holding them firmly in place, they can concentrate on filling and preparing their wings for flight.

RICK'S TIPS

Be Sure!

When buying plants from a retailer, always ask what type of pesticide may have been used on them. Some pesticides can stay in the soil and plants for months and end up killing your caterpillars.

Don't let sunlight shine directly through your magnifying glass, or it might burn your caterpillar, and your hand.

Outdoor Living

An alternative way to raise caterpillars is also a more natural solution, one that's possible if you're fortunate enough either to have host plants already available or to have included some in your garden scheme after the fact. Remember, caterpillars consume and frass, consume and frass, so with the right plants, you can simply place your larvae onto the host plant and then encase the entire plant in netting, securing it at the base with a cord. Your caterpillars will be able to pick and choose which branch is right for them. When it's raining or when predators are afoot, they can seek shelter amid the foliage.

Checking On Your Critters

The number of caterpillars assigned to each particular plant will determine how often the cord should be loosened and the droppings removed. Frass will often get caught in the small forks of branches, so give the plants a light shaking. While the netting is untied, check the plant for any chrysalises and unwanted insects, and remove both. The former are removed because mice eat chrysalises (and they will chew through netting); the latter because other insects will kill or eat caterpillars. The tied netting will safeguard against aerial assaults by dragonflies, ichneumon flies, or tachinid flies, not to mention praying mantises, ladybugs, lacewings, and a multitude of others.

Even when you have your air defenses in place and are ready for war, you still have to consider the possibility of a ground attack, but there's no need to raise the white flag in surrender. Commercial ant traps placed at the base of the plants should help, as long as they won't be inviting to inquisitive children or curious pets. The traps may get waterlogged during rain, so keep an eye on them.

The 1-inch-long (25 mm) Viceroy caterpillar eats the leaves of willow, poplar, aspen, apple, cherry, and plum trees.

No Bone to Pick Here

Butterflies have an **exoskeleton**. What we consider the skeleton is on the outside of the body. This body armor helps to protect them from falls and attacks by predators.

Pot It Up

An alternative to the in-the-wild method (and one that's easier for you and safer for your charges) is to keep host plants in pots, either terra cotta or plastic. The advantage of potted plants is that a thin smear of petroleum jelly around the circumference of the pot will deter creepy crawlies like ants from invading. Powdered charcoal or dried tansy leaves placed around the base of the plants will also discourage invaders.

A bonus to using potted plants is that they can be rotated: When they've been nibbled down, the caterpillars can be removed to a different plant. Then the "nibblee" can be placed back in the sunlight to recuperate. Once the plant is back to peak condition, it can again take its turn at being the guest of honor at a larvae luau.

Ideally, when covering potted plants with netting, use thin rods as a simple framework to protect the plants and keep the netting from resting directly on the leaves. Coat hangers will work, provided the plant isn't too tall. Whatever type of rod you use, bend it into a U shape, and then stick the two ends into the pot's soil. Repeat with another rod so that the intersection of the two Us forms an X at the top of the plant. Tie them together at that point.

Next, cover the framework and plant with the netting and secure it around the pot with a cord. The framework will allow better air circulation and a healthier environment for your babies. A nice, gentle breeze will actually blow away several disease-causing problems, whereas stagnant air will develop them.

This simple caterpillar cage is created out of netting, coat hangers, and a potted plant.

Making Caterpillar Cages

If you have extra space and time to donate to this butterfly undertaking, I recommend constructing 3-foot cubes out of wood or PVC, which will put you in the major leagues of butterfly farming. In a 3-foot by 3-foot cage there's plenty of room for everybody, so when chrysalis time rolls around, competition for space isn't a problem. Each larva will find a suitable place on the netting, where it can anchor and change into a pupa.

Do you have plenty of wood at your disposal? Then wood should be your material of choice. Wood does have a serious drawback, though: If a virus or killing protozoa develops, it will get into the wood and may never come out. Several coats of heavy-duty varnish will protect the surface from intruding infections, but the varnish will eventually wear off from repeated cleansings with bleach. However, if you keep everything tidy from the beginning and don't allow housekeeping to get out of hand, you should need to use only soap and water and not the stronger bleach.

PVC's advantages are that it can take many cleanings and that the surface won't harbor diseases as readily as wood will. Also, netting can be hot-glued right to the sides, and doors can be fashioned from flaps secured by Velcro strips. The finished PVC cage can be placed on a tabletop or construction blocks. Don't extend the side pieces to make them into legs, because they'll be too unstable in the wind. Plus, you'll want to support the bottom, since one or more potted plants will be placed into each finished setup.

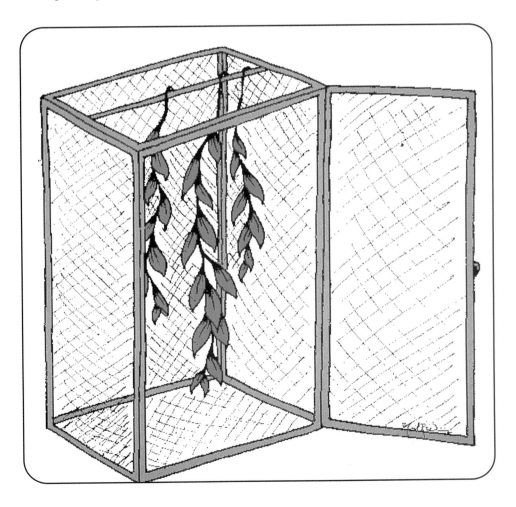

A 3-foot (90 cm) caterpillar cage can accommodate a dozen caterpillars at once.

Come and Get It

Caterpillars of the carnivorous Harvester butterfly eat woolly aphids. The female lays her eggs in the middle of aphid masses, and dinner is already waiting for her babies when they hatch.

Net Advantages

With either PVC or wood, the best netting to use is clear UV-treated netting, in as fine a mesh as is available — 32 by 32 will keep out just about all pests. If the clear type isn't available, 50-percent shade or less is preferred.

Too dark, and your larvae will think it's always night, while your adults won't want to mate. Also, without sufficient light, your nectar plants will stop producing nectar. Even a few days of overcast weather will cease the flow. So stay with the lower percentages of shading properties. You can always add additional shade later with a potted tree or shrub.

Some species, like the Swallowtails, prefer to lay their eggs on plants in dappled sunlight. This effect can be achieved by covering half of the cage with a piece of material so that it's partially sunny and partially shaded. If that's what Swallowtails want, that's what they should get, because it could mean the difference between no eggs and a hundred of 'em.

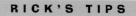
The percentage marking on mesh is the amount of light reduction provided by the netting material. For example, a 30-percent shade will let in 70 percent of available light; 40-percent will allow in 60 percent; and so forth.

Netting for a caterpillar cage must be made of fine mesh, but a butterfly net can be made of anything from fine mesh to old pantyhose.

The Maternity Ward

The designated maternity-ward cage is the one where you'll keep the fresh, healthy plants that pregnant mothers are always searching for. Since they can't fly away, they're forced to deposit their treasure onto the plants at hand. This system allows you to control exactly how many eggs are laid on each one. If your female seems reluctant to lay, give her some time to think things over. One trick that usually works is to remove her from the host plants and place her in a hanging cage that's in the darkest area available. In fact, total darkness works best. When she's removed 24 hours later, feed her just the sugar-water solution (a 10-percent solution of sugar water or a children's juice drink such as Juicy Juice), and put her back in the cage with the host plants. She'll usually make up for the lost time, even laying up to twice as many eggs per day than normally expected.

Once the host plant has a good number of eggs, remove it to the next cage.

The Day-Care Cage

Your children need to eat and play, and here they can safely dine and meander to their liking. When the time comes for them to molt, they'll simply climb up the sides of the cage and remain motionless. Don't move your caterpillar if it isn't moving by itself. They are very susceptible to injury at this point, and it's best to leave them alone. When molting is finished, they'll resume eating and creating mounds of frass.

Cocoon vs. Chrysalis

Moths spin a protective cocoon around themselves. The chrysalises of most butterflies, on the other hand, are bare.

Don't move a motionless caterpillar, such as this 2-inch (50 mm) Black Swallowtail. It may be in the process of molting and is vulnerable to injury.

The Baltimore Checkerspot has a striking 1-inch (25 mm) chrysalis.

Tending the Chrysalis

Once the chrysalises have been formed, they can be removed for safekeeping. Otherwise, if there are too many, the remaining caterpillars may bite the other chrysalises or knock them down.

Chrysalis Removal

Locate the area where the **cremaster** (a silken pad from which the chrysalis hangs) meets the netting. Then, using your thumb and forefinger as if to pinch it, gently grasp this silken pad. Gently pull slowly and steadily, and the silken pad will become a long thread. This thread can be wound around a pin or hook to be used for hanging in the emergence area.

Or you can do what has long been a favorite Yuletide tradition on our butterfly farm: Use Christmas ornament hangers. The silk can easily be wrapped around the hooks, which are then placed on the "chrysalis tree." With the right timing, the pupae will hatch on Christmas morning. See page 150 for more information.

This works only if you have a surplus of pupae species that can be kept in refrigeration until needed. It won't work with tropical species like the Gulf Fritillary or Zebra Longwing, but other species can handle prolonged cold. In fact, Tiger, Spicebush, and Zebra Swallowtails can be kept in the fridge for up to *two years.*

The broods of chrysalises that would normally overwinter have a natural antifreeze built into their systems, so they can easily tolerate the temperature of your refrigerator, which hovers at approximately 40º F. Just place the chrysalises in an airtight container and let them relax.

About 30 days before you need them, remove them from the fridge and let them warm up at room temperature. The warmer they are and the longer the **photoperiod** (a cycle of light and dark periods) the sooner they'll emerge. If kept at 80°F and given 18 hours of light, they'll hatch much faster than they would at 70°F and 8 hours of light. In other words, warmer and lighter usually means quicker, while cooler and darker means slower. This applies to all stages of development.

If you find a chrysalis, be sure to handle it with care and keep it out of the sun.

Romance among Butterflies

Females usually mate only once in their lifetime, but males can mate many times. In the field, many males adopt a perch and wait for females to enter their territory.

Mating

Not all chrysalises need to be removed from the cages. If chrysalises are left inside the cage, the emerging adults obviously have the opportunity to find each other quite easily. Females are capable of mating the day after they hatch, but males need a day or two before they are ready. Fortunately, they usually emerge before the females.

On the other hand, in captive situations such as your cages, mating is actually induced by fragrances the males emit called **pheromones,** which are released from special colon-shaped pouches on the wings. This intriguing gland, coupled with stunning ultraviolet colors reflected from the wings, will entice an unmated female to change her single status posthaste. When butterflies are confined to a small area, these pheromones will actually build up and cause a frenzy that incites mating, and it's not uncommon to find females that will mate more than once under these conditions.

Once mated, the female can be placed into the maternity cage, to lay her eggs in peace and quiet. The male, meanwhile, can be used many times for mating, but it's best if he gets a day or two of rest in between.

Swallowtails are more likely to mate naturally when their food plant is present to instigate the ritual. Plant these in pots, or simply offer a branch or two placed in water. A plastic gallon jug works just fine as a holder; the opening is small enough to prevent the butterflies from falling into the water. The female likes to alight on the plant from time to time to sample the potential baby formula. This will reassure her that the nursery is all set and everything will be okay.

Is She or Isn't She?

Some butterflies can be **dimorphic,** that is, show two different color forms. The Tiger Swallowtail female is most notorious for this. Some may appear chocolate brown or even black to fool birds into thinking that they're a less tasty species. But on close inspection, the telltale tiger striping can be seen on the underside of the forewing.

The male Monarch butterfly has a black spot, or scent pouch, on each wing. The female has no such spots.

Giving Nature a Hand: Hand-Pairing

With some species, like the Painted Lady, it's hard to keep them from mating. But with other species, if for some reason your best-laid plans go awry, you may need to play matchmaker by hand-pairing your butterflies.

The technique sounds difficult, but it can actually be quite easy. The most important rule: use opposite sexes. With your forefinger and thumb, take hold of each adult by the wings. Hold them as close to their shoulders as you can. Then, while holding them upside down, begin to lightly rub the tips of their abdomens together. The male will quickly open his claspers. Sometimes also referred to as valves, the claspers are not pinchers. They are used to take hold of the female during mating, and the grasp can be so strong that they can even fly in this position.

If you're successful, the young couple can then be placed into a cage to continue mating. If you're not successful, don't get discouraged. On the first attempt, one or the other may be a bit reluctant. But if you try a few times without any luck, return them to their cage, and wait a half hour. They may then surprise you and connect instantly on your next session.

The male butterfly grips the female with its claspers, seen here magnified to about three times their actual size.

With your forefinger and thumb, hold each adult by the wings. Holding the butterflies upside down, rub their abdomens together until the male opens his claspers and grips the female. When the male has clasped the female firmly, place the pair in an undisturbed spot for at least 15 minutes.

Which Is Which?

The Pieridae family, consisting of Whites and Sulphurs, exhibits the clearest distinctions between males and females. See pages 125 – 132 for specific details.

Problems and Solutions

If after this pause you still experience problems, place the male and female in total darkness for 24 hours. Then place the cage in normal indoor light. It may take a few minutes before they settle down. Once they do, feed them the sugar water solution and allow time for digestion. Leave them alone for the remainder of the day. Most butterflies seem to prefer mating in the afternoon, usually between 3 and 5 o'clock, although this timing isn't carved in stone, and every pair is different under different conditions. That's not to say that mating won't occur at any time; pairs have been found at 10 or 11 o'clock at night. It all depends on the receptiveness of the female.

Mating has to last for at least 15 minutes for the male to transport that sperm sac to the female. Also, keep in mind that the more often a male is used, the longer each session will last. Experienced males can take an hour or more to complete their task. There is no set timetable. But always remember that when using a male to mate with more than one female, give him a day of rest in between assignments.

If you find a pair that is deeply involved in the mating process and standing quietly, do not disturb them. If they are in a cage with other adults that are not mating, remove the others to a different place. If for some reason the others should get frightened or become too active, they may cause the breeding pair to unlock prematurely.

A mating pair should always be left undisturbed.

A Note on Inbreeding

A very important point to consider here is inbreeding. After three generations of inbreeding of a population, some genetic corruption will begin to take place. The first sign of inbreeding usually becomes visible with emerging adults, who will be reduced to almost half their normal size. Often, too, the adults will be sluggish and even have trouble curling and uncurling their proboscises. In severe cases they will show signs of albinism, emerging either as true or partial albinos. Some may be just a lighter shade than normal; others may be born white or with white patches. And without the proper coloration of their species, they may never find mates in the wild.

The solution is to introduce new breeding stock into the bloodline. The easiest way is to catch a free-flying wild adult and simply use it. If you've planted your garden as described in chapter 2, your yard is undoubtedly full of wild leps, so just take your choice, and swing your net.

If you catch a female, there's a 99-percent chance that she has already mated and is laying eggs. A male can simply be put in the vicinity of your females, and nature will tell him what to do. Once the wild insect is introduced and mated with your stock, the bloodlines will be strong and healthy again.

Wear quiet or camouflage colors when stalking butterflies and day-flying moths.

RICK'S TIPS

To get closer to butterflies, be careful of what you wear. Loud or brightly colored clothes will startle them. Also, many fabric softeners leave clothes with an ultraviolet aura or halo that animals and insects can spot a mile away. When going into the field, wear darker, subdued colors, but not black. Black is a no-no. Blues, greens, and camouflage will allow you to get much closer to your quarry, but a spicy tartan is a definite fashion disaster. And except for antitick spray around your ankles, you may want to skip other insecticides. The aroma will send leps running in every direction.

Quirks and Peculiarities

Some species of butterflies have individual idiosyncrasies regarding mating, feeding, or just staying alive. The following are a few of their traits that I've noticed along the way.

MONARCH ADULT

Monarchs

These beauties are fairly easy to breed (in a closed environment they'll happily mate over and over again) but egg laying may sometimes pose a problem. The solution could be as simple as changing the species of milkweed used for egg depositing. Many northeastern Monarchs may choose not to lay on southern milkweed species and vice versa.

Monarch caterpillars may be reared on artificial diets, but the emerging adults will be undersized and sluggish. If artificial diets are used, it's best to supply "real" food in the final instar prior to chrysalis. A difference won't be noticeable then.

RED ADMIRAL ADULT

Vanessas

Normally Vanessas are hard to keep from breeding. A 16-hour photoperiod will usually activate their pheromones, which is why they do so well in an indoor situation. This creates problems of a different sort. With Painted Ladies and Red Admirals, egg laying can go on for several weeks. And they aren't particular about where they lay their eggs. The side of a cage, paper cups, books — anywhere is fair game when they're ready to drop eggs.

Caterpillars do well on artificial diets (though sometimes they'll refuse to eat when temperatures fall below 75°F) and they emerge from chrysalises full size and very healthy. Vanessas are very actively sought after by schools for projects and can easily be sold at any time during their life cycle. This marketability makes them very desirable to rear.

RICK'S TIPS

Mating Practices

If your butterflies seem reluctant to mate, there are a few things you can try. Sugar water will stimulate the mating urge in butterflies. Males do need a fair amount of salts to stay prolific, but a sugar-water diet will cause mating to happen sooner. Fruit sugars have a tendency to slow mating down. In fact, they slow the critters down in general, which may actually prolong their lives by a few days or weeks.

Reluctant pairs can be kept in total darkness for 24 hours. The morning of their breeding they should be fed sugar water and placed in a bright room. *Do not place them in direct sunlight* or they will beat themselves silly trying to find the source of light. Most species will mate in a flight cage or atrium. Monarchs and Painted Ladies will easily mate in the hanging cage shown in chapter 3. They require little space and actually seem to do better in a confined situation. Host plants don't have to be present to induce mating.

Swallowtails

Flight cages are needed for Swallowtails. They need not be fancy. They can be the $50 screen houses at the discount store. A spare bedroom or basement will also do.

One trick to breeding Swallowtails is to offer the female host plants to taste, as well as nectar plants, which will inspire her to think she has found a home for her babies. Temperatures should be 75 to 80°F. Swallowtails can be hand-paired, but they have very fragile legs that will break off easily.

Also, Swallowtail caterpillars are finicky. They don't do well if their food is standing in water — this eliminates the soft drink/butter container idea in chapter 3 — because the additional moisture may cause infectious breakouts. Since the larval stage lasts for 4 to 5 weeks, take this into consideration when considering raising Swallowtails.

TIGER SWALLOWTAIL ADULT

Fritillaries

Frits are difficult to rear, though Great Spangled, Aphrodite, and Variegated Fritillaries can be used for local releases. They become stressed easily and don't travel well. They are hard to ship because they cannot stay in the releasing envelopes (see page 158) for long. The eggs are laid in the fall near violets and hatch in the spring, so it is hard to overwinter them.

Fritillary caterpillars feed at night on violets. They overwinter as tiny larvae and will give the appearance of dying on you, but the little critters are just sleeping.

ZEBRA LONGWING ADULT

Longwings

Despite the Fritillary name, some lepidopterists consider the Gulf Fritillary a member of the Heliconia family, along with other Longwing butterflies such as the Zebra Longwing and the Julia. Regardless of where they scientifically belong, they all do well in atria, breed easily, and release well.

But the Zebra does have its peculiarities. These butterflies use only passionflowers for their host, which need to be present for them to be induced into breeding. They also need a considerable-sized flight house to perform their prenuptial dance. And last, they don't travel well.

Heliconia enjoy warmer temperatures than other butterflies, so that will play an important part in causing mating to take place. They are very comfortable at up to 90°F. Egg laying is quite different with Longwings and can take place over many weeks or even months. Once a certain density is reached on a particular plant, egg laying will stop until a new plant is introduced.

Butterfly Atria

Once you've mastered the basic butterfly-raising techniques, it's time to take it to the next level: the private atrium. Atrium: The word just sounds so enchanting. Who wouldn't want one?

Easy Atria

The private butterfly house can be grandiose or extremely simple. You could start with a simple $50 screen "house," such as is usually available at any discount store during the warmer months. They are cheap, useful, and quite portable and will last for several years. Bonus: If you have a large area of host plants in the field, these bottomless structures can be placed directly on top. Then when your larvae have devoured the original section, the whole thing can be picked up and moved to the next spot. In colder climates where year-round outdoor rearing isn't possible, just fold the whole thing up, and pack it away until the following season.

If you want to spend a bit more, several companies have excellent models with aluminum-framed sides and heavy-duty mesh walls that will last for a decade. It may be all that you'll ever need. The bottom will also fit to the ground more snugly than the cheaper type. The flusher the fit, the less chance your space will be invaded by snails, ants, or mice. Some models even have locking doors and rubberized roofs. Most garden centers and do-it-yourself stores have many models on display for you to evaluate.

An inexpensive screen house is the perfect environment for your caterpillars and their host plants.

Grow, Grow, Grow

To accelerate the growing season, the house can be wrapped in standard packing bubble wrap or a swimming pool cover. Wrap the entire structure, but allow an opening for the door. The bubble wrap is a wonderful insulator that will let you start plants outdoors much earlier in the year than you normally could.

The atrium can also be outfitted with tables to hold the caterpillar and butterfly cages. If you intend to use tables to support your rearing or breeding cages, go simple and light. The legs and frames can be made from lumber or, better yet, plastic. Fashion the tops from wire mesh, not wood or metal. This is not to say you shouldn't use whatever is available, but if you have a choice, go with ½-inch-square wire mesh.

A solid wooden surface offers disgusting marauders like earwigs hideouts in between raids. You don't need them, so don't make it easy for them. Also, you won't have to worry if you overwater your plants because the excess can simply run off through the wire mesh. (Plant saucers, on the other hand, will collect overflow water that can become a death trap for your babies.) The mesh is also inexpensive and easy to clean. And, again, if diseases turn up, they may be harder to eradicate in wood.

Grow your host and nectar plants in pots. It's not a good idea to plant your flowers directly into the soil floor. Nematodes and other ground-dwelling vermin may take their toll on your plants before your caterpillars ever get to them. Furthermore, if your host plants are planted in the ground, once they've been eaten back by your larvae, they'll need replacing, which will require a lot more work. We're talking labor intensive here, and we don't like those words. Keeping your plants in pots means they can be easily rotated (i.e., replaced) as they're munched by hungry caterpillars.

Another reason to grow in pots is that if the butterfly house comes with a solid roof, the plants may not receive enough sunlight to produce nectar. Indoors, supplementing with sugar water is fine, but outdoors the sugar-water solution would be an endless buffet for ants. So plants grown in pots can be rotated out in the sun to replenish themselves.

Less Than Meets the Eye

A hot item in the marketplace is the pressure-treated gazebo. With strong wooden roofs, sturdy construction, and net windows, they're obviously the perfect butterfly house, right? Wrong! Sure, they look great and seem to have everything you need — for a price — but there are definite pitfalls.

First, the intricate inside-roof construction offers plenty of nooks and crannies for spiders and other predators to hide in. There are also lots of spaces for larvae to get lost in, and adults have a given talent for getting stuck in crevices. Further, the framed and netted sides don't let in a great deal of light, which may cause your plants to suffer. Lastly, look at the floor. Are there openings between the floorboards? If there are, consider them passages for ground-dwelling assailants just looking for an opportunity to enter an unlimited butterfly buffet.

Bottom line: Examine these gazebos very carefully before you spend your hard-earned money. If one meets the ticket, decide just how much space you're really going to need and go with that setup.

Atrium Option

Your butterfly abode can be fitted with very inexpensive misting systems. Costing less than $50, they can be programmed to go on and off several times a day. The duration of misting can also be set with the timer. With plenty of food available and a guaranteed shower every day, your little butterflies will be quite self-sufficient for a few days at a time. With your free time you may even want to venture out into the real world.

But then again, why would you want to? You've got it all right in your own backyard.

Marketing Butterflies

There is a big market for live butterflies right now, and an entire industry of people who just farm and sell butterflies. The biggest rage is releasing butterflies for weddings. As the newly married couple emerges from the church, their friends open special origami envelopes and release adult butterflies into the sky. The happy couple then walks underneath a canopy of swirling butterflies to the waiting limo.

Butterflies are so fascinating that many schools have included them in the science curriculum. Schoolchildren are then privileged to witness firsthand the miracle of metamorphosis.

In the last 10 years, just in North America, nearly 100 live exhibits and living butterfly zoos have opened for the public to visit. These are very popular with tourists, and the line waiting to get into an exhibit is usually quite long.

The curators of these exhibits and the teachers arranging the school projects need to acquire their butterflies from somewhere, and it could be from you. Once it is known that you can supply a live butterfly gift, everyone will begin calling you. I know. I have been making my living at it for 20 years. The nicest part about butterfly farming and marketing is that the livestock produced (your butterflies) is meant only to spread joy and never to be killed. Whenever you give another person a live butterfly you must always explain how to make a wish come true (see page 62).

Releasing Your Butterflies

The reason you started to raise butterflies in the first place is that you wanted more of them in your neighborhood. So now it's time to set them free. Most likely they'll stay within a few hundred yards of your home. As you sit in your garden and see a lovely winged piece of rainbow glissade by, smile. You've done well. Be proud of what you have created.

BALTIMORE CHECKERSPOT

Dos and Don'ts of Releasing Butterflies

There are many species of butterflies residing in every state. Enjoy and become acquainted with the ones that live in your area before you attempt to raise others. If they are not in your area now, it's because what they need to survive is not present.

With the signing of the Plant Protection Act, there is now a $50,000 fine for illegally transporting a butterfly across a state line.

- **Do** experience the excitement of raising butterflies.

- **Do** release your butterflies back into your garden.

- **Do** release them outside at the proper time of year.

- **Do** use only healthy and active butterflies.

- **Do** use butterflies from your home state.

- **Do** encourage others to nurture and release butterflies.

- **Do not** import live butterflies from other countries.

- **Do not** ship live butterflies out of your home state unless you have secured permits from the United States Department of Agriculture.

- **Do not** purchase live butterflies from breeders who do not have the proper permits.

- **Do not** release butterflies into an area where they would not naturally be found.

- **Do not** release butterflies at a time of year when they would not normally be flying.

- **Do not** collect butterflies from state or federal parks.

First Aid for Butterflies

If you find a butterfly with a torn wing, you can try carefully taping it with transparent tape. This will allow the butterfly to fly and possibly live out its normal lifespan.

CPR for Butterflies

If you find a weak or injured butterfly, try feeding it a diluted version of sugar water. Sometimes just fresh water will be enough. Place the patient's feet on a moistened pad that has been saturated with feeding solution. If the proboscis does not extend naturally, help it out by uncurling it with a toothpick. Carefully place the toothpick into the center of the curled proboscis. It will look like a coiled watch spring. Then gently uncurl it until it makes contact with the feeding pad. You may have to hold it in place for a minute or so before the butterfly begins feeding.

Once the drinking tube is extended, watch for any up-and-down pumping action of the proboscis. If no motion is detected, take the forefinger and thumb of each hand and hold the butterfly's front wings near the front edges. Hold each front wing, one between each set of your fingers, as close to the butterfly's body as possible. Begin to move the wings up and down in a flapping motion. This action may start the suction inside the proboscis and draw the needed food into your patient.

Taping a broken wing, as with this Orange-Barred Sulphur, may allow the butterfly to survive long enough to reproduce.

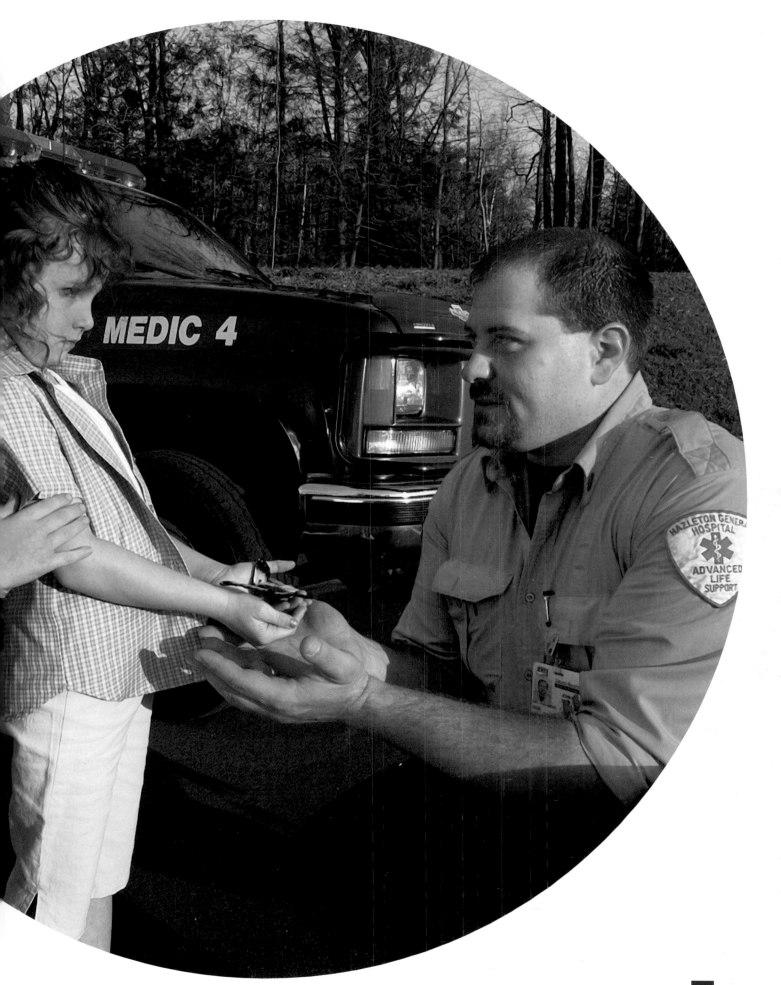

The Most Common Backyard Butterflies

What Was That?

It's a bird, it's a plane, it's a Great Spangled Whatchamacallit!

These days you can't turn around without seeing butterflies everywhere. Not just in the garden, mind you. They soar in the background of TV shows, jump out from magazine ads, alight on teenagers' hairdos, and perch on street vendors' jewelry carts. Obviously, you're not alone in your fascination with butterflies.

At this point, it would help if you knew a bit more of what you're talking about when you talk about butterflies. Whether it's a guest asking you to identify a multicolored flying streak zipping through the garden or a neighbor bringing you things in jars to identify, people are going to expect answers from you. And since you are now the neighborhood's official resident expert "Butterfly Person," they probably expect those answers to be right. Go figure!

On a cool day a butterfly may linger on your hand to enjoy your body heat.

Learning to See

When you're out butterfly hunting, it's easy to think you've witnessed the isolated flight of extinct species. This is especially true if you haven't done some preliminary research, such as reading a book. It's also easy to confuse related species, not to mention subspecies.

Identification can be a problem in the beginning, but don't worry; we'll work our way through this. With a little investigation you'll soon find that you should be looking for long tails, for example, or that the only difference between species X and species Y is some little black dash underneath the hind wing.

The following pages will help you identify the most likely suspects: 40 of the most common North American butterflies. When using this guide, allow a little latitude in interpretation. Photos provide an exact rendition of the subject creature, but you will discover that, in real life, not all butterflies are exact replicas of each other.

Keep in mind that the color variations within a species can be quite dramatic. These variations can be caused by a number of things, including diet, temperature, or a limited or corrupted gene pool. Here are some examples.

Different species of Swallowtails can look very similar, such as this Tiger (top) and this Anise (below).

- Some species may live in a microenvironment of only a few hundred square yards. (Then it's safe to say that their family tree has very few branches!) That small population might develop specific, distinctive markings that don't appear in photos in any books.

- Humidity and moisture can play a part in color and size. A wet winter or summer will produce more vivid colors than will drier conditions.

- What and where they eat can affect the color, size, and even shape of caterpillars, chrysalises, and adults. Northern species can vary from Southern ones.

- The seasons can also govern physical attributes. Adults that emerge early in the spring may be smaller or larger, depending on the species, than their offspring emerging later in the year.

The important thing to keep in mind here is that the Spicebush in my garden may not look like the Spicebush in yours. And be sure to look closely, because maybe it isn't even a Spicebush after all but actually a dark-phase Tiger.

Confused yet? That's to be expected. Trust me, with time and patience it will all get easier. Before you know it, you'll have actually earned your reputation as the resident expert.

Seasons and Life Stages

In your observations you'll find that some species may be in the adult stage and flying at only limited times during a particular season. The remainder of the year they're still present but in a different life stage. If butterflies aren't on the wing when you are, search for their other forms. I can pretty much guarantee you'll begin to find them. For this purpose, photos and illustrations of eggs, caterpillars, and chrysalises have been included in the identification section and throughout this book. Variations in physical characteristics can occur in any stage of the butterfly's life, so allow a little bit of leeway in matching up critter to picture. Don't give up if they're not exactly alike. Instead, get excited!

Finding a New Species

If the butterfly that you discovered doesn't match the pictures here, maybe you should get excited rather than disappointed. After all, you have as much chance as the next person to be the one to discover a new species. It isn't unthinkable to stumble across an unnamed butterfly living on your property. So if your newfound treasure doesn't quite match up to the picture, it's time to investigate further. You just may be on to something.

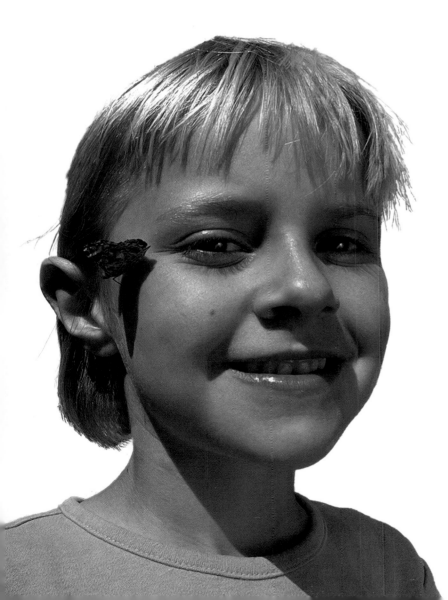

What to Bring on a Butterfly Expedition

If you plan to chase some butterflies through a meadow, it's best to wear long pants, tucked into socks, and regular shoes, boots, or sneakers (not sandals). If you live in tick country, apply bug spray or rub the leaves of pennyroyal, a natural tick repellent, around your ankles. Here are some more essentials:

- Butterfly net (see p. 40)
- Magnifying glass
- Camera
- Sunblock
- Hat with sun visor
- Journal or notebook
- Field guide

What's in a Name?

As you become more involved with your new passion, you'll stumble into something as scary to you as any predator is to your butterflies: scientific Latin names. Now, before you dismiss them as completely unnecessary, consider that as you branch out, you'll begin to converse and deal with people worldwide. And this may lead to a problem.

Most butterflies are known by a common name. These are the names you learn as a child and assume everyone else uses, too. Guess again. A Mourning Cloak in the United States and Canada is a Camberwell Beauty in the United Kingdom. But if you say *Nymphalis antiopa,* not only will everyone know what you're talking about, but you'll actually sound as if *you* know what you're talking about. And if sounding like a bona fide lepidopterist isn't a bonus, I don't know what is.

So take the time to learn the scientific names. That way, if you say *Nymphalis antiopa,* anyone deeply involved with butterflies will know what you mean, whereas they may not have a clue about a regionalized moniker like Mourning Cloak.

Understanding Scientific Names

Scientific names consist of two parts. Take that Mourning Cloak, *Nymphalis antiopa.* The first, capitalized word indicates the genus, a class of organisms with a similar structure or evolutionary history. Others in the *Nymphalis* genus include the California Tortoiseshell *(Nymphalis californica)* and the Compton Tortoiseshell *(Nymphalis vau-album).* The second, lower-case word indicates the species ("antiopa"), a class of organisms that are so genetically similar that they are capable of interbreeding.

After a brief exposure to standardized scientific names, you'll quickly begin to see which butterflies are closely related. So just relax and trust that it will all eventually make sense to you as you see how indispensable this nomenclature is in getting to know your butterflies. For now, just read through this section without worrying about retention. The names will still be here when you want them.

The Swedish naturalist Carolus Linnaeus was responsible for devising the process of scientific naming. His book, *Systema Naturae,* published in 1758, began the formalization of names used today. And the system has been used for this long for one simple reason: It works.

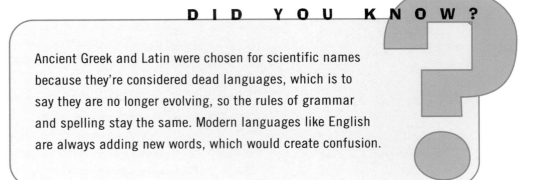

DID YOU KNOW?

Ancient Greek and Latin were chosen for scientific names because they're considered dead languages, which is to say they are no longer evolving, so the rules of grammar and spelling stay the same. Modern languages like English are always adding new words, which would create confusion.

Name Pronunciation

A few basic tips will help you in your name recall. First of all, remember that all vowels are pronounced. The type of accent above the vowel will tell you whether it's long or short. The accent marks I have added are to help you pronounce the words more easily. You won't see them listed in this manner in most reference books, but they are here to help you. Once you are familiar with the pronunciations they will become second nature to you.

- Two vowels written together but pronounced as one are called a *diphthong*.
- All Lepidoptera family and subfamily names end in the most common of all diphthongs: ae, which is pronounced as a long E (i.e., *ee*).
- With consonants, the letters *c* and *g* are the problems, to wit:
    When *c* is followed by *ae, e, oe, i,* or *y,* it has a soft *s* sound.
    When *c* is followed by *a, h, o, oi, or u,* it takes on the hard sound of *k.*
    When the letter *g* is followed by *ae, e, oe, i, or u,* it's pronounced hard, as in "go."

Now that your head is thoroughly spinning, let's clear it by identifying some butterflies, shall we?

How to Look at a Butterfly

When you spot a butterfly in your garden, first make note of its overall size, color, and shape. Here are some things to look for.

- Is it huge, stamp-sized, or in between?
- What color is it?
- Are the twin tails of the Swallowtail present (p. 95)?
- Are the wings sharply angled, as in the Question Mark (p. 111) or Comma (p. 112)?

If the butterfly lets you look closer, try to notice stripes and patterns.

- Are there any dots of color near the inside edge of the hind wing?
- Is the wing edge different from the center part?
- Are the wings the same on the upper surface and on the underside?

Is it a Mourning Cloak or a Camberwell Beauty?

Lepidopteran Gallery

This gallery of butterflies does not follow the old format of "This must go here and that can't go there." It was arranged to allow enjoyable browsing with a touch of pizzazz. These 40 butterflies were chosen because they are either highly visible or have interesting or unusual habits. I hope they will lead you deeper into the amazing world of these "flying flowers."

The big and splashy Swallowtails begin the parade, because folks love to see colorful and exotic things. Once you see how magnificent these creatures are, all the others will start to reveal themselves as subtle works of airborne art.

Following the Swallowtails come the workhorses of the group, the Brush-footed. Many schools now raise, tag, and release Monarchs for the University of Kansas, or study the metamorphosis of Painted Ladies in the classroom as part of their science curriculum. You can find the other members of this group by searching fields and gardens. The species described here are only a small sampling of the 150 members of this group.

The Gossamers are smaller, delicate, and easily overlooked. With about 100 species they are common, like the Brush-footed, but less conspicuous. From a distance they may seem plain, but given the chance they will fascinate anyone with their intricate patterns. Gossamers are hard to catch and even harder to hold onto, but they are well worth watching.

All those yellow butterflies are called Sulphurs, and every region of North America can brag about its particular residents. Because of their color they are very visible and easy to spot. From the tiny Pink-Edged to the huge Orange-Barred, all Sulphurs are delightful. There are about 22 different Sulphurs in North America.

Like the Sulphurs, Whites can be localized or widespread, depending on the particular species. Just don't disregard them all as Cabbage Whites. They could just as easily be Mustard, Veined, Great Southern, or Pine Whites. If you decide to keep a checklist or tally sheet, the Sulphurs and more than a dozen different Whites will quickly add numbers to your list.

Skippers may not be the prettiest butterflies on the block, but there are a lot of them out there — nearly 250 species in North America. Their stubby bodies, less-than-spectacular colors, and smaller size don't place them high on the popularity chart. They prefer edges and openings, but with the right inducements they will visit gardens. Listed in the gallery are three of the more common Skippers.

The Neotropicals will not be available for everyone to see, but they were included because it is hard to believe that such exotic-looking leps reside in North America. They are beautiful to watch and do wonderfully in captivity. So there is no need to travel to the tropics to see something unusual, when they are already here. Any vacation to the Gulf States should include a search for Zebras, Gulfs, and Malachites.

The final two butterflies are odd to say the least. The Harvester (actually a Brush-footed) has unusual dietary requirements, and the Snout has a unique appearance. Certainly not as showy as the Neos, they are still quite fascinating. They will, I hope, stimulate further study of all butterfly habits and quirks.

SWALLOWTAILS AND PARNASSIANS
Papilionidae
(pap-ill-ee-ON-ah-dee)

The most noticeable thing about Swallowtails is the clublike projection extending from the hind wing. Some species have two or more of these decoys, which are used to thwart predator attacks. The thin, bobbing tail looks very much like the insect's head to a hungry avian aggressor, but with a stoop, a swoop, and a snatch, the disappointed bird returns to its perch with only a bit of wing to show for its trouble, not the anticipated meal. The tails unfortunately do not grow back as with some reptiles, nor do the missing appendages inhibit flight. Generally, after surviving an attack, the Swallowtail can go about its daily business.

Swallowtails are usually larger butterflies with showy colors, and they number a little over two dozen varieties in North America. Every section of the country can enjoy a certain type of Swallowtail. The Eastern Tiger is the most noticeable of all and covers a wide range extending into Alaska. California can boast of the Two-Tailed, and the Southwest can carry on about the beauty of the Three-Tailed. Folks along the East Coast may enjoy the greenish opalescence of a passing Zebra Swallowtail, but they may never witness its Northwestern cousin, the Oregon. The tailless Parnassians, which are generally white and black with a dash of red here and there, love cold weather and high elevations, preferring mountain meadows to your garden.

If you see a large, lumbering butterfly in the field, it most likely will be a Swallowtail. Many species of Swallowtails never stop flapping their wings when hovering at a flower to nectar. This is is a Palamedes Swallowtail.

All Swallowtail caterpillars share one trait. An **osmeterium,** a retractable organ located behind the true head, emits a foul smell (harmless to humans) that renders them less than palatable to predators.

If you're fortunate enough to find any Swallowtail larvae in your garden, try this experiment. Gently and carefully squeeze the caterpillar behind the head, or apply pressure to its back. The osmeterium will quickly be exposed: a fascinating sight.

Giant Swallowtail *Papilio cresphontes*

Look for the green, orange, and often yellow eggs on the leaves of citrus in the South and on hop tree, prickly ash, and rue in the North.

The larvae are large and mottled brown with a creamy white saddle and smudges at the back end. Length: 2½" (60 mm)

The Giant does everything slowly. When it's finally ready to pupate, it will become a grayish brown chrysalis with yellow and brown patches near the wing section.

WINGSPAN AVERAGE 4½–6" (100 mm)

The largest of all the North American swallowtails, the Giant Swallowtail has enormous wings that take it from the Gulf States through the Midwest and well into Canada. The black forewings are lined with two rows of yellow spots that converge near the wing tip. There is only one row of spots on the hind wing. The yellow underside is trimmed in black and looks like a photographic negative of the upper surface.

At every stage, the Giant Swallowtail is sizable. The larvae can reach a length of two and a half inches (60 mm). Their insatiable appetite for citrus trees has made them a scourge in Southern states, where they are considered a pest and called "Orange Dogs." The chrysalises are also large, often more than an inch and a half (40 mm) long.

Host plants: Citrus, hop tree, prickly ash, rue
Nectar plants: Lantana, orange

Pipevine Swallowtail *Battus philenor*

WINGSPAN AVERAGE 3" (75 MM)

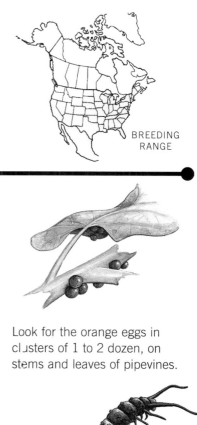

BREEDING RANGE

Look for the orange eggs in clusters of 1 to 2 dozen, on stems and leaves of pipevines.

The dark purplish brown caterpillar has two gruesome filaments projecting forward. Despite its fearsome appearance, it is a gregarious creature. Length: 2" (50 mm)

Eventually the larva will change into a tan or green chrysalis suspended by a girdle filament.

The Pipevine is a work of art and sure to impress anyone fortunate enough to see it. Although it is found throughout the United States, it isn't fond of the northern Rockies. And if some form of *Aristolochia*, or pipevine, such as Dutchman's pipe or Virginia snakeroot, isn't present, the Pipevine won't be, either.

This is a lovely creature. The blue iridescent sheen of the upper surface of the hind wing is the perfect complement to the ebony forewing. From the underside the Pipevine is just as impressive, with large orange spots set against a field of blue. The Pipevine is one of the few butterflies that lays its eggs in clusters.

Because of its preferred diet, the Pipevine is thought to be distasteful by birds and not readily attacked. It also seems that many other swallowtails capitalize on this by imitating the Pipevine's coloration and thereby gaining protection from predators.

Host plants: Dutchman's pipe, knotweed, pipevines, Viginia snakeroot, wild ginger

Nectar plants: Azalea, honeysuckle, orchid

Spicebush Swallowtail *Papilio troilus*

BREEDING RANGE

Look for the pale green eggs primarily on leaves and stems of spicebush, but also on sassafras and bays.

The dark green caterpillar has the typical orange and black eyespots that are associated with swallowtail larvae. Length: 1½" (40 mm)

The chrysalis can be green earlier in the season or bark-colored if formed later in the year. Adults that emerge in the spring are smaller than those of the later season.

WINGSPAN AVERAGE 4" (100 MM)

In some areas, the Spicebush is also referred to as the Green or Green Clouded butterfly, because the males have a greenish tint to their hind wings. The females can be distinguished from the males by their bluish hue. The forewing is black with a single row of white spots on both the top and the bottom. The underside of the hind wing is a collection of wonderful orange-red spots surrounding a blaze of blue.

Throughout Eastern North America, the Spicebush can be found patrolling wooded paths and abandoned roads. Here it can feast on Joe-Pye weed, jewelweed, and honeysuckle. It will also be quite happy to visit a garden plot. Because it is easily confused with the unpleasant-tasting Pipevine Swallowtail, birds often leave it alone.

Host plants: Spicebush, sassafras, various bays (*Persea* spp.)
Nectar plants: Joe-Pye weed, jewelweed, lantana, honeysuckle

Eastern Black Swallowtail *Papilio polyxenes*

WINGSPAN AVERAGE 3" (75 MM)

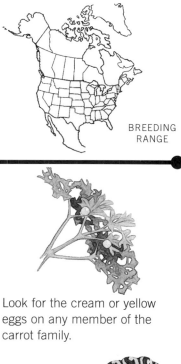

BREEDING RANGE

Look for the cream or yellow eggs on any member of the carrot family.

If you live east of the Continental Divide and have any member of the carrot family growing in your garden, you will probably have Black Swallowtail butterflies. They are a beautiful harmony of black and blue, with dots of orange and edgings of white on their wings. (The western counterpart is called the Anise Swallowtail because it feeds on anise plants.) And guess what's been eating your parsley and dill (along with Queen Anne's lace and other members of the carrot family)? It is the Black Swallowtail caterpillar.

Smaller than most North American Swallowtails, the Eastern Black is still big on beauty. Intricate patterns of white, yellow, and orange dots decorate its velvety black wings. Females and males are a bit different. The hind wings of the female have more blue than those of the male. In addition, the males have two rows of yellow spots on their wings. On the little ladies these are muted white spots that look as if they have been smudged.

As with all Swallowtails, the caterpillars have a defense mechanism called an **osmeterium.** This bright orange organ looks like a snake's tongue and emits a foul odor, protecting the caterpillar from being eaten.

The Black Swallowtail can be found east of the Rockies from Canada to Mexico.

Host plants: Carrots, celery, dill, parsley, Queen Anne's lace, rue, Texas turpentine broom

Nectar plants: Milkweed, phlox

The caterpillar will go through color and pattern changes as it progresses from one instar to the next. Newly emerged caterpillars are black with a white saddle. They soon develop a vertical green-black stripe directly behind two yellow eyespots. Length: 2" (50 mm)

Chrysalises vary from green to brown, depending on the surface they are attached to. Those formed on a rough surface will be brown, while those set onto a smoother surface will be green.

Eastern Tiger Swallowtail *Papilio glaucus*

BREEDING RANGE

Look for the yellow-green eggs deposited on the leaves of willow, birch, tulip, and cherry trees.

The caterpillars are masters of disguise and at first look like brown and white bird droppings. Eventually they become smooth green larvae, resembling small snakes with orange eyespots directly in front of a thin yellow-black neckband. Length: 2" (50 mm)

The green or brown chrysalis is always suspended from a twig.

WINGSPAN 3⅛–5½" (80–140 MM)

If you have lilacs, you have Tigers. You couldn't keep them away from lilacs with a tennis racket. This bright yellow butterfly with ebony stripes can be found wherever lilacs grow throughout the eastern United States and Canada, and even in Alaska.

The female Tigers are sometimes dimorphic, meaning that they have two different colorations. A female may emerge from her chrysalis as chocolate or black, instead of the familiar bright yellow, and the characteristic tiger stripes will barely be visible on the undersides of the wings. It is believed that this is a protective device to fool birds into thinking that these females belong to a less tasteful species, such as the Pipevine Swallowtail, which most birds will try to avoid.

The emerged larvae are difficult to find because they prefer to feed in the canopies of the treetops. So, unless you are extremely tall, they may be hard to locate.

Host plants: Many broadleaf trees and shrubs, including lilac, willow, birch, tulip, and cherry

Nectar plants: Bee balm, buddleia, honeysuckle, sunflower

Zebra Swallowtail *Eurytides marcellus*

WINGSPAN AVERAGE 4½–6" (100 MM)

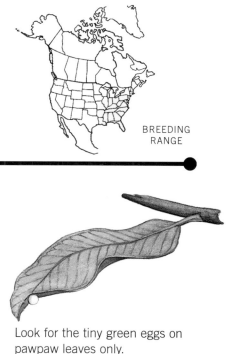

BREEDING RANGE

Look for the tiny green eggs on pawpaw leaves only.

The caterpillars may exhibit either of two color variations, light green or dark. The green version has one black stripe at mid-hump and is circled in thin bands of yellow. The dark form has a white band at mid-hump and is encircled with white, black, and yellow stripes.
Length: 2" (50 mm)

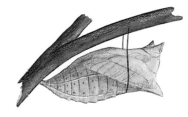

The chrysalis is a short and robust little barrel that looks as if it is about to explode.

To watch a Zebra Swallowtail glissade effortlessly through the canopy is one of the great thrills of butterfly watching. A member of the Kite family, it has wings that are more triangular and tails that seem longer for its body size than those of the other Swallowtails. The white wings are boldly striped with black and gracefully flow into white tails with black centers. Two red dots and a few blue ones decorate the upper wing surfaces, while from underneath a beautiful scarlet stripe bisects the hind wings. The entire package is wonderfully presented with an opalescent green iridescence. Adults that emerge early in spring are smaller overall and paler than those born later in the year.

If you are fortunate enough to live in an area that supports pawpaw, search out this masterpiece. It will be well worth your efforts.

Host plants: Pawpaw
Nectar plants: Milkweed, asters, red clover, zinnia, cosmos, lantana, pentas, daisy

BRUSH-FOOTED BUTTERFLIES
Nymphalidae
(nim-FAL-ah-dee)

If you see an orange or mostly brown butterfly darting around your garden, it's probably one of the Brush-foots. If it lands and keeps its wings half open, chances are even better that it's one of these *Nymphalidae.* This is a White Admiral.

This large and diverse family numbers more than 150 species just in North America. They include the Fritillaries, Anglewings, Admirals, Checkerspots, Tortoise-shells, Longwings, Crescentspots, Vanessas, and Leafwings. They are called Brush-footed because the forelegs are reduced and useless for walking and are used instead to clean the palpi and proboscises.

Medium to small in size, these leps are generally a shade of orange or brown, though some can be quite colorful. Because it's such a large group, the larvae of the family vary in color as much as the adults do. Their lifestyles are also varied and not consistent within the family as with the Swallowtails. Some members of this group overwinter as adults, while others prefer to spend the cold months in the safety of the chrysalis or will chance it in the caterpillar stage.

All Nymphalidae are powerful fliers, as is demonstrated by the long flights of the Painted Ladies and Red Admirals. Unlike the Monarch, however, they are not considered true migrants, because they do not make a return trip. Repopulation is carried on by their offspring the following summer.

From time to time this group has members added or subtracted from the lineup as the powers that be decide that things have been too simple for too long. They stir things up and regroup. When they can't get out to play with butterflies the experts get itchy and change names just to keep everyone else on their toes. And they even do it in Latin to make it all the more confusing to the poor soul that only wanted to know "What in the world was that?"

Milkweed Butterflies

Danæidae

(dah-NAY-ah-dee)

Medium- to large-sized and powerful fliers, these members of the Brush-footed family eat plants belonging to the genus *Asclepias*. This dietary staple leaves them a bit distasteful and sometimes poisonous to birds, but they give fair warning to potential attackers by announcing their threat with their orange and black colors. A natural warning pattern in nature, this color combination can deter a hungry predator before it's too late for the butterfly.

There are four Milkweed butterfly species in the United States: the famous Monarch, the more southern Queen, the even more southern Soldier, and the most southern of all, Tropical Milkweed or Large Tiger. The last two are found only in the extreme tips of Texas and Florida.

Many unrelated species, such as the Viceroys, are said to gain protection by imitating the colors of the milkweed butterflies. Viceroys seem to be the second most recognizable species after Monarchs, because they are always used as an example to explain mimicry within butterflies in basic biology textbooks. Viceroys are generally smaller than the Monarchs, but the size of all butterflies can be affected by outside circumstance, such as a sudden depletion of available food. Oddly, a strain of white Monarchs can be found living on the campus of the University of Hawaii in Honolulu.

The Queen, like the Monarch, is a true milkweed butterfly. After dining only on milkweed, the caterpillars become toxic to birds. They advertise this with their bright colors. Other butterflies, such as the Viceroy, gain protection from predators by mimicking the coloration of the Queen and Monarch.

Monarch *Danaus plexippus*

WINGSPAN AVERAGE 4½–6" (100 MM)

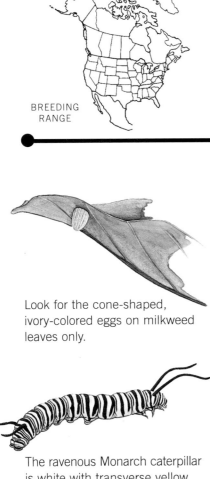

BREEDING RANGE

Look for the cone-shaped, ivory-colored eggs on milkweed leaves only.

The ravenous Monarch caterpillar is white with transverse yellow and black stripes and long black filaments at either end. Length: 2" (50 mm)

The smooth green chrysalis is dotted with gold and crowned with a golden circle.

The familiar orange and black wings of the Monarch have made it the most widely known butterfly in North America. Famous for its unbelievable migration, this lep is fascinating at any stage.

The egg is found only on species of milkweed. In a few days the black head of the larva will appear at the tip of the egg. It will soon eat its way out and begin a legendary journey.

The caterpillar dines only on milkweed, which is toxic to many organisms and makes the cat toxic, in turn, to predators. Its vivid yellow, black, and white color pattern is thus a danger signal to predators. Long filaments at either end of the larva are used to flick away parasitic flies and wasps. Unfortunately, they are not the best defense, and many caterpillars become infected and die.

The exquisite green chrysalis is found suspended upside down. Near the top of the smooth-skinned capsule is a golden circlet trimmed in ebony. Toward the bottom are golden dots with two at the very apex. These are said to become the eyes of the adult. Just prior to emerging, the entire chrysalis will become clear enough that the complete adult will be visible.

Monarchs that emerge near the Autumnal Equinox are known for their spectacular fall migration to Mexico. Male Danaidae have a large black dot in the center of each hind wing. These are scent-releasing pouches, which are used during courtship to excite the female.

Host plants: Milkweed
Nectar plants: Milkweed, asters, red clover, zinnia, cosmos, lantana, pentas, daisy

Viceroy *Limenitis archippus*

WINGSPAN AVERAGE 3" (75 MM)

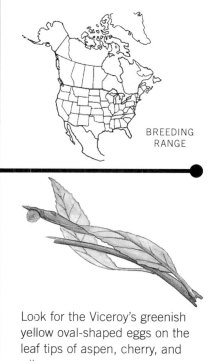

BREEDING RANGE

This bold butterfly can be found just about anywhere in the United States, though it's more likely to visit the rotting fruit in your garden than the flowers. Famous for its mimicry of the Monarch, the Viceroy is a troublemaker wherever it turns up. It has been the source of many an argument over the years, because we still don't fully understand it. Scientists haven't come to a consensus on which form of adaptive mimicry it uses for defense. In the northern states that are predominantly occupied by Monarch butterflies, the Viceroy takes on the more common orange color. But where the Queen butterfly is more prevalent, Viceroys can be found in darker shades of russet brown. Either color tricks predators into thinking it's one of these less palatable milkweed-eating leps.

Obviously, it's easy to confuse the Viceroy with the Monarch or the Queen; however, it offers a very visible clue to its true identity. Across the midsection of the Viceroy's hind wing runs a black line as thick as one of the many veins. Also, the Viceroy is usually a little smaller than the Monarch. However, size alone can't be a deciding factor in identification because in drought years, when host plants dry up prematurely, many Monarchs and Queens will be smaller than usual and can easily be mistaken for the Viceroy.

Here are two more tips. At rest, the Viceroy keeps its wings partially open; the Monarch and Queen keep theirs closed. On the wing, the Viceroy reveals its identity through its flight pattern of flap, flap, glide. The other two species fly as if they had a purpose.

Host plants: Willow, poplar, aspen, apple, cherry, plum
Nectar plants: Milkweed, asters, red clover, zinnia, cosmos, lantana, pentas, daisy

Look for the Viceroy's greenish yellow oval-shaped eggs on the leaf tips of aspen, cherry, and willow.

The caterpillar can be brown or green, but it always has a small white saddle on the middle of its back. Even at this stage it's a mimic, often resembling bird droppings. The caterpillar spends the winter months in a structure of rolled-up leaves referred to as a **hibernaculum**. Length: 1¼" (30 mm)

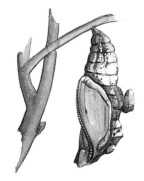

The chrysalis, like the caterpillar, looks like bird dung.

Red-Spotted Purple *Limenitis arthemis*

BREEDING RANGE

Look for the tiny green eggs on the leaves of many small trees.

Looking more like a bird dropping than an easy meal, the cream caterpillar has a humped back with a darker saddle. From behind the caterpillar's head extend two bristle-covered stubs. Length: 1½" (40 mm)

The pupa is whitish gray with dark streaks and silver marks, but the saddle and abdomen are brown.

WINGSPAN AVERAGE 3¼" (80 MM)

Easily confused with the Spicebush and Pipevine Swallowtails, the Red-Spotted Purple does not have a tail. Its darting flight and zigzag patterns allow it an easy escape through the woods long before you can identify it. It is fond of basking on the tops of shrubs or by roadside puddles, which is usually the only time when you will get to enjoy its real beauty. On the hind wing is a magnificent halo of iridescent blue. In the center of the hind wing is a field of blue surrounded by a blue crescent at its margin. The outside margin of the forewing, meanwhile, is covered with white and red dots. The reddish brown underside is complemented by a wonderful blend of red and orange spots and two rows of blue chevrons.

Wherever it roams in eastern North America, the Red-Spotted Purple will be found just as easily on dung, rotting fruit, or even carrion as it will in gardens.

Host plants: Apple, aspen, cherry, hawthorn, hornbeam, poplar, willow
Nectar plants: Milkweed, asters, red clover, zinnia, cosmos, lantana, pentas, daisy

Great Spangled Fritillary *Speyeria cybele*

WINGSPAN AVERAGE 3" (75 MM)

BREEDING RANGE

Look for the tan-colored eggs near violets in late summer.

The nocturnal-feeding larvae are black with black-tipped orange spines covering their backs. Length: 1⅓" (35 mm)

The chrysalis is a mixture of muted browns, often with a reddish hue.

The Great Spangled is the largest of all Fritillaries in North America, and its wings may span nearly 4 inches. With such large wings, the Great Spangled Fritillary is capable of great flights and boasts an impressive range, from the southern United States north into Canada.

Its typical blend of oranges, sienna, and burnt umbers are common to the group, and its upper wings are marked with black dots, chevrons, and lines. The underside of the forewing is a replica of the top, though with more buff overtones. The hind wing exhibits the telltale silvery spots of a true Frit.

Once the caterpillar emerges from its egg, it will eat its own eggshell and then hibernate for the winter. Several months later, it will wake from a long winter's nap to find fresh food, in the form of violets, awaiting it.

Host plants: Violets
Nectar plants: Milkweed, asters, red clover, zinnia, cosmos, lantana, pentas, daisy

Variegated Fritillary *Euptoieta claudia*

BREEDING RANGE

Look for the ribbed, cream-colored eggs on passionflowers, pansies, violets, stonecrops, and plantains.

The very striking reddish orange larva sports six rows of dark spines that protrude from white lines running the length of the sides. Length: 1¼" (30 mm)

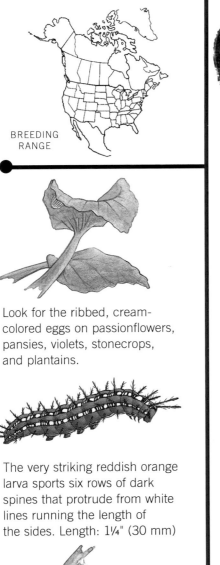

The chrysalis is a shiny blue-green, appearing as if it were constructed from mother of pearl. Adorned with flecks of gold, orange, and black, it looks more like a piece of jewelry than a pupa.

WINGSPAN AVERAGE 2" (50 MM)

The Variegated, whose tawny wings can be seen throughout most of North America, is the missing link between the Gulf and the Common Fritillaries. The black zigzag pattern and black spots are consistent with the typical Frit pattern, but the Variegateds lack the silvery spots generally associated with their larger cousins. The larvae have a more diverse menu, including the passionflower favored by the Gulfs.

Regular visitors to gardens, Variegateds will just as eagerly visit carrion and manure. They hibernate over the winter in the southern tier, but not in the more northern extent of their range.

What the Variegated Fritillary may lack in attractiveness in the adult stage is certainly made up for in the other phases of its life.

Host plants: Violets, pansies, stonecrops, passionflowers, plaintains
Nectar plants: Meadow flowers, hibiscus, composite family

Meadow Fritillary *Boloria bellona*

BREEDING
RANGE

WINGSPAN AVERAGE 1½" (38 MM)

Look for the greenish yellow eggs exclusively on violets.

The purplish black Eastern Meadow caterpillar is covered with brown, branching spines and marked with dark chevrons and dashes inside two yellow lines. The caterpillar hibernates when it is half grown. The larva of the Western Meadow is gray with dorsal lines, reddish side stripes, and red spines becoming black toward the black head. Length: 1" (25 mm)

The Eastern and Western Meadow Fritillaries are easily found along roadsides and damp meadows throughout the central and northern tier of North America. Their orange wings are less than two inches across and display the black dashes and dots characteristic of Fritillaries. Like the Variegateds, they lack the silvery dots on the underside of their wings that are present in their relatives.

Because of their smaller size they can easily be overlooked, even though they can be quite numerous in a single area. Not exceptionally highflying leps, they tend to stay closer to the vegetation, where the males can show off for the females.

Host plants: Violets

Nectar plants: Meadow flowers, composite family

Eastern Meadow pupae are brown to yellowish brown with gold marks near the abdominal area. The Western chrysalises tend to be browner and are white at the midsection.

Mourning Cloak *Nymphalis antiopa*

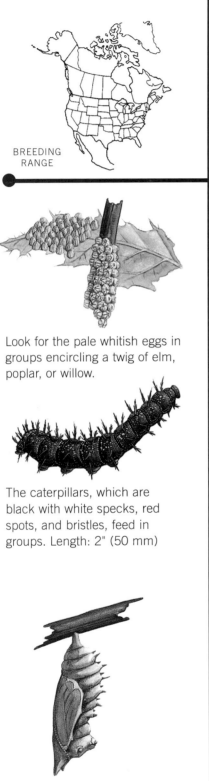

BREEDING RANGE

Look for the pale whitish eggs in groups encircling a twig of elm, poplar, or willow.

The caterpillars, which are black with white specks, red spots, and bristles, feed in groups. Length: 2" (50 mm)

The chrysalises are suspended upside down. They vary in color from tan to bluish black, with bumps tipped in pink.

WINGSPAN AVERAGE 3¼" (80 MM)

Brownish maroon wings edged with cream can mean nothing other than Mourning Cloaks. The hibernating adults are usually one of the first leps on the wing in spring. Their angled upper wings are dotted with blue and exhibit a lovely iridescent sheen, but from below they are wonderfully camouflaged. Although they are the largest of the Tortoiseshell family, they can still easily hide when perched on the side of a tree. When approached, they emit an audible click, and with a flash of color they are gone. The Camberwell Beauty, as the Mourning Cloak is called in the United Kingdom, prefers mud and fruit to garden flowers, but don't count it out as an early season visitor.

Unlike most other butterflies, Mourning Cloaks are communal. The female lays eggs in masses that may encircle a twig. This carries on into the caterpillar stage, and the larvae are quite happy to feed in groups. When a mass of feeding caterpillars is disturbed, all of the cats will move in unison. This is a most interesting thing to observe in the field. Mourning Cloaks can be found almost anywhere in North America.

Host plants: Elm, poplar, willow

Adults prefer: Rotting fruit, dung, meadow flowers

Question Mark *Polygonia interrogationis*

BREEDING RANGE

WINGSPAN AVERAGE 2½" (60 MM)

Look for the long green eggs on the leaves of elm trees, nettles, or hops. The eggs are laid in groups and often stacked vertically, one on top of the other.

The rusty orange caterpillar is sprinkled with white dots, with two black spines at the head and orange spines everywhere else. Where there aren't spines, there are orange and yellow lines. Length: 1½" (40 mm)

This dandy midsized butterfly received its name from the silver question mark found on the underside of its hind wing. It is worth searching it out just to see it. As on the other Anglewings, the scalloped wings and earthy color allow it to hide easily when motionless. The upper wing surfaces are a somber orange marked with dashes and dots of black. The undersurfaces are mottled hues of browns and tans. But as plain as it may sound, the entire wing is bordered with lavender.

The chrysalis is only a temporary summer home for the Question Mark because, like the other Anglewings, this lep prefers to spend the winter as an adult, hibernating under loose bark on trees or hollow logs. This feat allows it to be one of the first butterflies on the wing in the early spring.

Host plants: Elm, hackberry, hop, nettle
Adults prefer: Rotting fruit, dung, meadow flowers

The sedate, grayish brown chrysalis hangs disguised as a leaf.

Green Comma *Polygonia faunus*

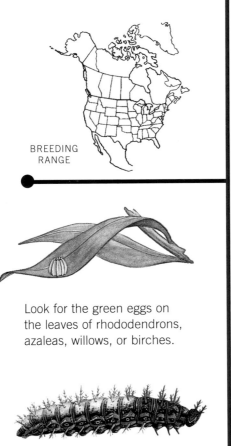

Look for the green eggs on the leaves of rhododendrons, azaleas, willows, or birches.

The larvae can be reddish or yellowish brown to tan with a white saddle, situated above the thorax, and whitish spines extending from orange lines. Cream, black, and orange lines complete the pattern. Length: 1¼" (30 mm)

The chrysalis is variable and ranges in color from tan to dark gray. It usually has gold spots.

WINGSPAN AVERAGE 2" (50 MM)

Various forms of Comma butterflies reside in North America, but the most widespread is the Green. This butterfly goes to great extremes to keep you from seeing it. The heavily angled wings are dull orange with brown spots and black borders set off by a thin, broken outline of yellowish tan. The undersurface of the wing is a mosaic in shades of grays with silver streaks. One of those streaks forms a silver comma on the hind wing. This special combination of colors allows the butterfly to blend into tree bark when it is at rest. Coloration does vary greatly in this species, however, and the Green Comma becomes smaller and grayer as it approaches the northern edge of its range in Alaska.

Host plants: Rhododendron, azalea, birch, willow
Adults prefer: Dung, fruits, puddles

Red Admiral *Vanessa atalanta*

WINGSPAN AVERAGE 2" (50 MM)

BREEDING RANGE

Look for the barrel-shaped, green eggs on nettle leaves.

The black larvae vary greatly and appear in combinations of yellow, brown, or black with touches of white or yellow. Whatever the chosen color pattern, these caterpillars prefer to live in the rolled-up leaves of their host plant and may even decide to hibernate inside. Length: 1¼" (30 mm)

With an identity all its own, the Red Admiral, once called the Alderman butterfly, is always a welcome sight. Its red wing patches and swift and erratic flight are keys to its identification. Territorial as this species is, it can still be found worldwide. In the Northern Hemisphere, it is found from Alaska to Mexico and Florida to Ontario.

The Red Admiral has orange semicircles on its upper wing surfaces, which make it recognizable anywhere. If it ever decides to take a rest, the camouflage patterns on the underside help it blend beautifully into its wooded background. As the predator approaches, it is startled by a flash of orange and one "gone" butterfly. Despite Red Admirals' various defense mechanisms, they are attracted to fermented fruits and tree sap and will readily come to baited traps.

Host plants: Nettle, false nettle, hop
Nectar plants: Cosmos, milkweed, Indian blanket

The small, brown chrysalis is flecked with gold and has small protuberances around the middle. It is usually found not on nettles but on the nearby stems of another plant.

Painted Lady *Vanessa cardui*

Look for the light green or yellow eggs on the leaves of members of the mallow family.

The color of the caterpillars can vary greatly, especially the color of the branched spines covering their backs, but usually a broken yellow line runs down the sides of the abdomen. The larval period can be quite short, depending on temperature and light. Length: 1¼" (30 mm)

The chrysalis can be tan to gray, accented with golden dots.

WINGSPAN AVERAGE 2¼" (55 MM)

Vanessa, also called the Thistle Butterfly, may be one of the most widespread of leps, showing up everywhere except the harshest of environments. The Painted Lady will emigrate in large numbers to occupy less populated northern areas, but the flights are usually in only one direction. Some adults may hibernate in areas with milder winter conditions, while others may choose to return south.

From above, the adult's wings are covered with blotches of orange and brown. The forewings exhibit the swash of pink for which the Painted Lady was named. They are tipped in black with white dots inside. The hind wings are edged with orange and black and have four blue-centered eyespots, circled in faint yellow. American Ladies (see opposite) have only two of these eyespots. The underside of the wings is covered with swirls of grays and grayish browns.

Host plants: Members of the mallow family
Nectar plants: A wide variety of garden and field plants

American Painted Lady *Vanessa virginiensis*

WINGSPAN AVERAGE 1¾ – 2⅛" (50 MM)

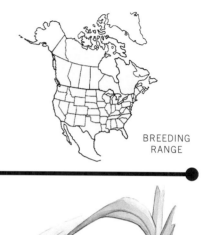

Look for the yellowish green eggs on the leaves of daisies, burdocks, and everlastings.

The black caterpillar is lined with yellow cross bands, alternating with branching spines and red and white spots. The caterpillar creates and feeds on a loose web of buds and leaves. Length: 1⅜" (35 mm)

The gold-speckled brown chrysalis can usually be found inside a web on the host plant.

This little burst of orange, black, and white can easily be confused with the Painted Lady *(Vanessa cardui)*. The two are similar in color and pattern, but there is one easy way to tell them apart. Look at the underside of the hind wing. If you see two blue-haloed eyes on each wing, it is an American Lady. If four smaller eyespots are found, it's the Painted Lady. If you spot three medium-sized blue eyespots, then you have found a West Coast Painted Lady.

Found in cooler climates than its cousins, the American Painted Lady has only two broods per year. American Ladies enjoy a wide range and are regular visitors to garden flowers. Also known as the Virginia Lady and the Hunter's Butterfly, it is as at home in an inner-city container garden as it is in open fields or along a streamside path. Although its range encompasses the entire continental United States and extends into Canada, you are more likely to find it in the East.

The larvae encase the buds and blossoms of their host in a loosely woven web and dine on them at their leisure. They will usually then pupate within this nest.

Host plants: Daisies, everlastings, and other composites
Nectar plants: Burdock, daisy, everlastings, mallow, yarrow, zinnia, heliotrope

Buckeye *Junonia coenia*

BREEDING
RANGE

Look for squat, dark green eggs on the leaves of any number of garden and field flowers, such as plantain, stonecrop, verbena, and snapdragon.

The caterpillar is black and spiny, with two rows of orange along the sides. Length: 1¼" (30 mm)

The chrysalis, which can be tan to mottled brown, appears to be sprinkled with cream-colored flecks.

WINGSPAN AVERAGE 2¼" (55 MM)

Two large, blue eyespots on tawny wings can only mean a Buckeye. No other North American butterfly has such pronounced **ocelli,** or pretend eyes, on its wings. These are used to startle or fool predators into thinking that the Buckeye is something that it is not. The forewing has two short, vertical, red-orange bars running through the center, while the hind wing has an orange border along the margin. This lep is an impressive sight when the sunlight hits it just right, for the iridescent colors seem to cast a halo over the entire wing surface.

From underneath, the Buckeye is extremely well camouflaged. From this point of view, the top eyespot, which is clearly visible, resembles the eye of a bird.

Buckeyes can be found throughout most of the United States and parts of Canada during the summer months, but as the cold approaches, they head south for the winter, sometimes in big migratory flocks. The following year the northern states are repopulated with their children and grandchildren.

Host plants: Plantain, snapdragon, stonecrop, verbena, other garden flowers

Nectar plants: Indian blanket, lantana, cosmos, clovers

Baltimore Checkerspot *Euphydryas phaeton*

WINGSPAN AVERAGE 2" (50 MM)

BREEDING RANGE

Look for clusters of the orange eggs on turtlehead, plantain, and false foxglove.

The larvae are rust-colored and marked with black bands between the segments. Older caterpillars show more black, with orange stripes down the sides. All stages are covered with black bristles from end to end. Length: 1" (25 mm)

The chrysalis is just as attractive as the adult butterfly, being white with black markings and orange bumps.

The Lord Baltimore butterfly was named for Governor George Calvert in the seventeenth century because its color matched the colors of the Calvert family crest. Common east of the Rockies, the Baltimore is a delight to find. Its crazy patchwork wings of orange, white, brown, and black make it a very attractive lep. Despite its small wingspan, it is spectacular and fun to watch. Baltimores range throughout much of eastern North America, demonstrating quite a size difference from one region to the next. Southern individuals tend to be larger than their northern cousins.

Interestingly, the caterpillars will feed on their host plant from inside a silken nest. They overwinter when half grown and resume their lives with the return of spring.

Host plants: Turtlehead, false foxglove, plantain, white ash
Nectar plants: Lobelia, purple coneflower, Indian blanket

Pearly Crescentspot *Phyciodes tharos*

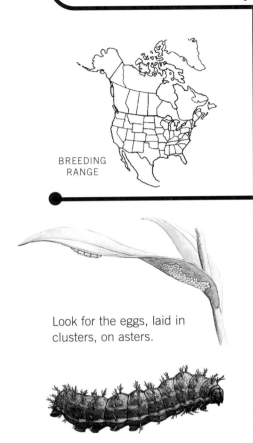

BREEDING RANGE

Look for the eggs, laid in clusters, on asters.

The brown or black caterpillar is covered with yellow dots and yellow bands along its sides. It also has branching spines, which may be yellow or yellowish brown. The larvae feed together but never construct a web, as do other gregarious species. Length: 1" (25 mm)

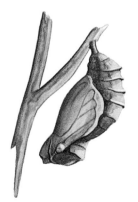

The chrysalises can be yellow, brown, or gray, but they all have stripes and patches of various other colors.

WINGSPAN AVERAGE
1¼" (32 MM)

Old Pearly is probably one of the most common of all the meadow butterflies. Even though the flight pattern is very low, where it could easily hide among the local vegetation, it is no "scaredy-cat" and will quickly attack anything that invades its territory. If all is judged to be safe, it will quickly retreat to its daily duties. The orange wings are a patchwork of black patches and zigzags. The underside of the forewing is pale orange with some black patterns, but the hind wing is a mixture of cream, tans, and browns.

Living throughout much of North America, Pearly Crescentspots are just as happy in your garden as in the field. Take the time to visit with these small but amusing leps.

Host plants: Asters
Nectar plants: Zinnia, daisy, clovers, goldenrod

GOSSAMER WINGS
Lycaenidae
(lie-SEEN-ah-dee)

Spring Azures and Tailed Blues often emerge from a winter's sleep long before other butterflies do.

About 100 species of these small butterflies reside in North America. They include the Blues, Coppers, and Hairstreaks and the Harvester (see page 142). Gossamers hold their wings closed over their backs when at rest. The females have six fully developed legs, while the males have reduced forelegs.

The sluglike caterpillars of the Gossamer family have some unusual features. Some species dine on flowers and buds as readily as they do leaves. Other species emit a sweet liquid called "honeydew" from glands on their backs. This liquid is relished by ants, who will protect and care for the caterpillar almost as if it were a domestic cow.

The caterpillars of the Blues and Coppers produce a honeydew liquid, which is consumed by ants, from glands on their backs. The ants, in return, protect the larvae from predators. This photograph of a Silvery Blue caterpillar being tended by an ant has been magnified to twice its actual size.

Great Purple Hairstreak *Atlides halesus*

Look for the eggs on mistletoe.

Covered with fine orange hairs, the caterpillars are greenish with a dark back stripe and faint yellowish side stripes. Length: ⅝" (15 mm)

The larva overwinters in a chrysalis of muted browns marbled with black.

WINGSPAN AVERAGE 1½" (38 MM)

It's hard to mistake the Great Purple for any other lep. Found throughout much of the United States, this butterfly displays beautiful sheens of blue, violet, and green as it darts about in the sunlight. But underneath it is brownish charcoal, to blend into the background and avoid detection. Two long filaments extend from the hind wing to divert attacks away from the head. On the underside near the body are red spots that complement the scarlet lower half of the abdomen. In general, the males are brighter than the females, but both show a black border along the upper surface of the wings. This margin is wider in the females, dulling their overall appearance.

The larvae quite happily eat the leaves of mistletoe. This makes the Great Purple a beneficial butterfly, since mistletoe is a parasite to many trees. Normally, the Great Purple will stay near the range of its host plant, but it has been sighted at various places along the U.S.-Canadian border.

Host plants: Mistletoes
Nectar plants: Daisy, purple coneflower, clovers

Gray Hairstreak *Strymon melinus*

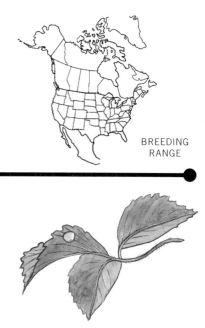

Look for the pale green eggs on cotton, mallows, strawberries, mint, and legumes.

The larval colors range from pink to reddish brown or even shades of mauve, but they always have green or white side stripes. Covered with fine brown hairs, the larva is more like a grub than a caterpillar. Length: ½" (12 mm)

WINGSPAN AVERAGE
1⅛" (29 MM))

The Gray is probably the most common of all the Hairstreaks in North America, but it's usually overlooked because of its small size and less-than-spectacular color. Also called the Cotton Borer, it can be found throughout the United States and is often considered a pest because of its large numbers.

The name *Hairstreak* originated from the thin lines on the underside of the wings. Fine filamentlike projections protrude from the hind wings like tails and act as defense mechanisms: These tails are mistaken for the antennae of the intended victim and break off easily when grabbed by a predator, allowing an opportunity for escape.

Though fancying cotton, mallows, and strawberries, the larvae have been reported to use up to 50 different species of plants as host.

Host plants: Cotton, mallows, strawberry, legumes, mints

Nectar plants: Yarrow, meadow and edge flowers

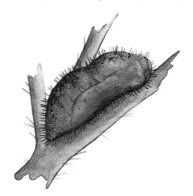

The pupa is a mixture of brown and black in which the larva hibernates to emerge early in the spring.

American Copper *Lycaena phlaeas*

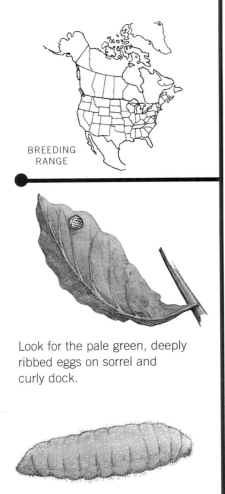

BREEDING
RANGE

Look for the pale green, deeply ribbed eggs on sorrel and curly dock.

The caterpillar may be either green or yellowish green with red side marks, or reddish with yellow side marks. Regardless of color, the larvae hibernate when only half grown. Length: ⅜" (10 mm)

The light brown chrysalis often has a reddish tinge.

WINGSPAN AVERAGE
1" (25 MM)

This hardy little butterfly is every bit as charming as the large leps of North America. Favoring the eastern half of the continent, the American Copper is sometimes called the Small Copper for obvious reasons. The group received its name from the coppery sheen cast by the wings.

The forewings of the American Copper are rusty orange bordered with brown, and the hind wings are brown bordered with rusty orange. Underneath, the wings are mostly grayish with some black dashes. This little creature would most likely be encountered in meadows and weedy areas, where it can more easily find its host plants, sorrels and curly dock. In your search for the American Copper, you will undoubtedly encounter other varieties of Coppers that inhabit your area, which adds to the fun of new experience and discovery.

Host plants: Sheep sorrel, curly dock, mountain sorrel
Nectar plants: Daisy, dandelion, clovers, milkweeds

Tailed Blue *Everes comyntas*

WINGSPAN AVERAGE
1" (25 MM)

BREEDING RANGE

Even after people get involved with butterflies they often overlook the smaller ones, and that is a shame. The Tailed Blue is a fabulous little chip of lapis with intricate patterns of black dashes and orange spots. There are two varieties: the more distinctively marked eastern and its paler and larger western counterpart. Although it is one of the earlier harbingers of spring, the Tailed Blue, with a wingspan of only an inch, is easily missed.

The most interesting parts of this butterfly are the delicate tails that extend from its hind wings. As the butterfly perches on a flower to nectar, the tails twitch dramatically, making it look more like a head than a tail. Would-be predators misguide their attacks to this area, and the Blue can escape and live for another day.

Host plants: Clovers, beans, peas
Nectar plants: Daisy, dandelion, clovers, milkweeds

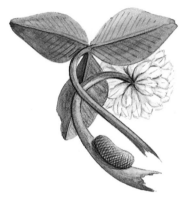

Look for the eggs inside flower buds and along the stems of clovers, beans, and peas.

The larvae are green, covered with a fine down. Those in the eastern U.S. have brown stripes running down the side, and western varieties have purple stripes. The caterpillars will overwinter inside the seedpods of their host plants. Length: ⅜" (10 mm)

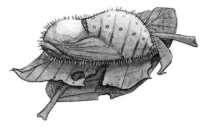

The tan or cream chrysalis also has the fine down of the larva.

Spring Azure *Ceslastrina ladon*

BREEDING
RANGE

Look inside nasturtium and dogwood flowers for the eggs of the Spring Azure.

The caterpillars vary considerably in color from cream to reddish, while some can even be shades of green. They have a green or brown line down their backs. Length: ½" (12 mm)

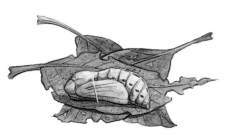

As with the caterpillars, the color of the chrysalis varies and also changes with the time of the year. Earlier chrysalises are lighter than the later forms.

WINGSPAN AVERAGE
1" (25 MM)

The Spring Azure, or Common Blue, is one of the first butterflies to be found on the wing in spring. These bursts of powder blue darting up from a wooded walk always provoke smiles. Tiny, for sure, but what they lack in size they make up for in cuteness. Take the time to observe their intricate patterns of silvery gray decorated with black and red spots. The adults that emerge early in the season are darker than those that are born later. They can be found throughout North America.

The differences in colors among the caterpillars are caused by surrounding influences, such as the season and geographical location. The larvae have a fascinating trait: They secrete "honeydew" through an opening on their backs and are thus often protected by ants, who savor the liquid. It is a nice relationship, where the larvae can safely go about their daily routine, and the ants get a free meal. The system works!

Host plants: Blueberry, California lilac, dogwoods, meadowsweet, viburnums

Nectar plants: Coltsfoot, daisy, milkweeds, other meadow flowers

This Cloudless Sulphur has just emerged from its chrysalis.

SULPHURS
Pieridae
(pee-AIR-ah-dee)

The Sulphurs are hard to miss because of their brilliant yellows. They are common all over North America. The most interesting are the Dogface Sulphurs. The yellow and black of the Southern Dogface can be upstaged only by the pink and black of its West Coast cousin.

With the exception of the Giant and Orange-Barred, Sulphurs are usually small- to medium-sized. Adults have six fully developed legs and are agile flyers. These chunks of sunshine will be just as at home in the garden as in the meadow, but many will prefer fields, weeds, and grasses for egg laying.

The Pink-Edged Sulphur is native to Canada and the northern United States. The female lays eggs on various species of blueberry, but it nectars from many flowers.

Cloudless Sulphur *Phoebis sennae*

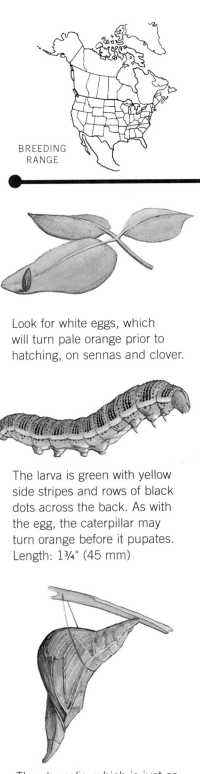

BREEDING RANGE

Look for white eggs, which will turn pale orange prior to hatching, on sennas and clover.

The larva is green with yellow side stripes and rows of black dots across the back. As with the egg, the caterpillar may turn orange before it pupates. Length: 1¾" (45 mm)

The chrysalis, which is just as impressive as the other life stages, is an extremely angular triangle of pink or green that changes colors as it matures.

WINGSPAN AVERAGE 2½" (65 MM)

The Cloudless Sulphur is also called the Giant because of its massive size, and the large yellow wings make it quite spectacular. Its leisurely flight patterns are best described as bouncing or bobbing and often appear to have no rhyme or reason. The Cloudless can be found in the eastern two-thirds of North America, and its late-summer flights will take it north into Canada. The lemon yellow males are brighter than the slightly darker females. The females also have a dark-colored, slightly off-center dot on the upper surface of the forewing.

The wonderful gigantic wings of the Cloudless can be seen in open areas and gardens, though they are equally at home in a southern cityscape. Wherever they decide to wander, they are a welcome sight.

Host plants: Senna, clovers, other legumes

Nectar plants: Hibiscus, cassia, pentas, bougainvillea

Clouded Sulphur *Colias philodice*

BREEDING
RANGE

WINGSPAN AVERAGE 2" (50 MM)

Look for the chartreuse eggs
underneath clover leaves.

The bright green caterpillar has a
dark stripe on its back and light
stripes along its sides. Length:
¾" (20 mm)

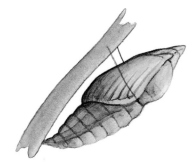

The small green chrysalises will
overwinter in the northern part of
their range.

These wonderful blasts of flying sunshine will make anyone's day. Medium-sized and lemon yellow, this lep is quite common throughout the United States and Canada. If the wings have sharp black borders, then it is probably a male. The borders of the females are not as pronounced and often seem to be smudged. The shading may extend over the entire wing surface to some degree and cause it to appear very dark. Just to add a bit more confusion to the situation, the female can be very pale yellow to even white. She can easily be mistaken for the Alfalfa, Dogface, or Cabbage White female. In addition, Cloudeds, or Commons, as they are sometimes called, will interbreed with the Alfalfa, which results in many pattern variations between the two.

If you see the female in a meadow, bobbing from clover to clover, then she is laying eggs. She will have several broods a year. Because the larvae have quite a taste for garden vegetables, many of them will be destroyed before pupating.

Host plants: Clovers and other legumes
Nectar plants: Clovers, dandelion, phlox, milkweeds

Orange Sulphur *Colias eurytheme*

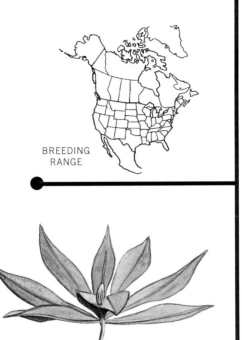

BREEDING RANGE

Look for the long white eggs on or under the leaves of clover, alfalfa, and a variety of garden plants, including lupines.

It's hard to distinguish between Orange and Clouded Sulphur larvae, but occasionally the Orange cats have pink stripes low on their sides.

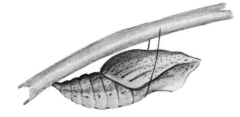

The green chrysalis is usually flecked with yellow or black.

WINGSPAN AVERAGE 2" (50 MM)

If you think you saw an orange streak go by, it was probably this ubiquitous little critter. Also called the Alfalfa Sulphur, it can often be found alongside Common Sulphurs and, in fact, the two sometimes mate to produce hybridized part-orange, part-yellow butterflies.

Adult male Orange Sulphurs have a distinct black border on the wing margins, with the rest of the wing being a splash of orange. But the amounts of black and orange are meaningless to females — who themselves exhibit a great variation in color due to crossbreeding — for they choose a mate by the ultraviolet reflections of a suitor's wings.

Host plants: White clover, alfalfa, vetch, lupine
Nectar plants: Clovers, dandelion, parsley, zinnia, other meadow flowers, members of the composite family

Dogface *Colias eurydice*

WINGSPAN AVERAGE 2" (50 MM)

If there was ever a butterfly that could bring a smile to young or old, it would have to be this little "flying pansy," the Dogface. The wonderful forewings exhibit the striking profile of a dog's face. It is debatable whether the forewings are yellow with black markings or black with yellow markings. The hind wings are lemon yellow with a faint margin of black, which may be broken up and appear as chevrons. From underneath, the wings are all yellow with a white-centered black dot on the forewing and a white-centered pink dot on the hind wing.

Of the two Dogface butterflies that reside in the United States, the California variety is the prettiest. It is California's state insect and even appeared on a United States postage stamp in 1976. The hind wings are the typical yellow of sulphur butterflies, but the forewings are tinted with rosy pink and bordered with black. The Southern Dogface is yellow and black, and the canine profile is easier to see. The famous face is not present on the female.

Both species have two broods a year. They will either hibernate as adults or overwinter in the chrysalis. The colder the winter, the rosier will be the blush on the California species' forewings.

Host plants: False indigo, clovers, lupine, vetch, leadplant
Nectar plants: Clovers, thistles, most composite flowers

Look for the yellowish green eggs, which turn crimson prior to hatching, on leaves of clovers, false indigo and, occasionally, leadplant.

The larvae are green with hairy bumps. Other markings vary greatly but usually involve some arrangement of stripes and dots of yellow, black, or orange. Length: 1" (25 mm)

The pupa is usually bluish green, becoming yellowish green near the abdominal area. Often it is streaked with white.

The Cabbage White may be the most prolific butterfly in the world, ranking right above the Painted Lady.

WHITES
Pieridae
(pee-AIR-ah-dee)

Ask most people to name three butterflies and they'll say the Monarch, the little white thingy in my yard, and those big yellow ones. The little white thingies are just that, the Whites. Those big yellow ones are Sulphurs. The Whites and Sulphurs make up the family Pieridae. Some of the almost 60 Pieridae species in the United States are considered pests, since they tend to eat garden vegetables.

Too many people assume that the Whites must be moths, because everyone knows that butterflies are beautifully colored. So at the sight of a White it's time to lock up the woolen sweaters before they get eaten. Wrong! Whites do pose a problem to garden vegetables, but not to your union suit.

Children may want to encourage the raising of Whites in huge numbers, because they consume Brussels sprouts and other unwelcome table fare. They are delicate and hard to handle but loads of fun for children to chase after. Often the Whites are the first butterflies to be noticed in the spring.

The male Whites and Sulphurs are prone to "puddling." A group of males gather at a shoreline, mud puddle, or bare patch of ground and drink the dissolved salts and minerals, which benefit their reproductive capabilities. Some species will interbreed, and variations in colors are very common.

Cabbage White caterpillars feed on cabbages, radishes, and nasturtiums so voraciously that they are considered pests.

Checkered White *Pontia protodice*

WINGSPAN AVERAGE 1½" (38 MM)

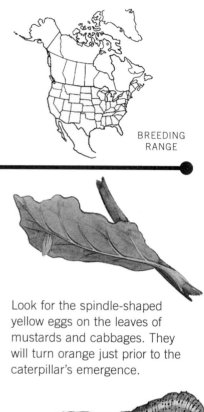

BREEDING RANGE

Look for the spindle-shaped yellow eggs on the leaves of mustards and cabbages. They will turn orange just prior to the caterpillar's emergence.

The caterpillar is bluish green, with lengthwise yellow stripes sprinkled with black. Length: ¾" (20 mm)

Checkered Whites can be found throughout most of the United States but do not make it all the way to the far northern tier or into Canada. The color patterns vary greatly, but the checkered design is always present. Those born in spring have more pronounced markings than their later siblings. Summer males may be all white without any checkering. Regardless of the time of year, they may have gray, olive, or tan tints overall.

The reproductive habits of this lep are fascinating. Since males do not produce a pheromone for mating, the way many butterflies and moths do, they attract females by their lack of reflected ultraviolet rays. The male's wing pattern absorbs ultraviolet light, and the female's reflects it. The pattern of the female is usually more pronounced than that of the male.

In the northern part of their range, Checkered Whites will be quite happy to overwinter in the chrysalis stage, but they will stay on the wing year-round in California.

Host plants: Crucifers, cleome
Nectar plants: Dandelion, Indian blanket, purple coneflower

The chrysalis is also blue-green and sprinkled with black and can be found overwintering in the northern part of the range.

Cabbage White *Pieris rapae*

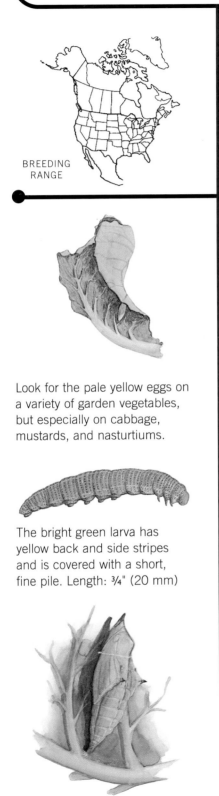

BREEDING RANGE

Look for the pale yellow eggs on a variety of garden vegetables, but especially on cabbage, mustards, and nasturtiums.

The bright green larva has yellow back and side stripes and is covered with a short, fine pile. Length: ¾" (20 mm)

After a very brief period, the caterpillar becomes a green, gray, or mottled brown pupa.

WINGSPAN AVERAGE 1½" (38 MM)

This invasive little pest is probably the most prolific butterfly going. It was introduced into Quebec from Europe in 1860. Escaping its captors, it can now be found everywhere in North America. A female is capable of laying nearly a thousand eggs in her lifetime. Although it has a taste for Brussels sprouts (which makes it a friend in my book) it's considered an agricultural pest.

Hardy and yet fragile at the same time, it is usually one of the first butterflies noticed at the arrival of warmer weather. Because of its all-white, somewhat dull appearance, it's often mistakenly referred to as the Cabbage Moth. Although it may be easy to mistake it for a moth, it's one of the easiest butterflies in which to identify the sexes. The males have one black dot in the center of the forewing; the female has two.

Cabbage Whites live everywhere, making them easy to find. This also makes them great candidates for children to raise. A piece of cabbage in a container will keep it happy, and the short life cycle will hold the interest of younger kids.

Host plants: Cabbage, mustards, and other crucifers; nasturtium
Nectar plants: Many garden and meadow flowers

TRUE SKIPPERS
Hesperiidae
(hes-per-EYE-ah-dee)

The caterpillars of this group, such as this Silver-Spotted Skipper, are green and tapered and have a fondness for grasses and weeds.

Skippers often get short-changed in the appreciation department. They are small butterflies and usually not considered very attractive. They deserve closer inspection because they can be quite interesting, with nearly 250 species residing in North America. They appear to be a cross between butterflies and moths because they are small, robust, hairy, and not very colorful. They can be seen everywhere in North America, along roadsides and in meadows, but they will gladly visit gardens.

Their habit of resting with their wings open adds to their similarity to a moth. To increase the confusion, some will rest with their forewings together but their hind wings flat. So what is a budding lepidopterist to do? Check the antennae for the telltale fishhooklike curve to the end section (as described in chapter 1). Also, Skippers have six well-developed legs. If still in doubt, watch them fly: They're named for their fast flight pattern, which resembles a stone skipping across the surface of a lake. Something small that bounces along the edge of a clearing is most likely a skipper. While not huge by any stretch of the imagination, and not beautiful by most people's standards, Skippers are every bit as interesting as any of their cousins.

In the field, adult Skippers can best be identified by their flight pattern as they bounce about a roadside or country meadow.

Silver-Spotted Skipper *Epargyreus clarus*

BREEDING RANGE

Look for the green, spherical eggs on legumes, locusts, and wisteria.

The yellowish green caterpillar has two orange eyespots on the enlarged brown head typical of skippers. The larvae prefer living in rolled-up leaf shelters, which they construct. Length: 1½" (40 mm)

Unlike other butterflies, the dark brown pupa is encased in a loose cocoon among leaf litter.

WINGSPAN AVERAGE 2" (50 MM)

Having one of the most extensive ranges of all the butterflies, the Silver-Spotted is equally at home in your garden or in a wooded setting. The dark brown forewings are marked with yellowish orange spots in the center. The unmarked hind wings are a uniform brown. From the underside, the golden spots show through the forewing, but the hind wings display the distinctive silver patches. This is an identifying mark that will separate it from others in the field.

Host plants: Beans, beggar's tick, licorice, locusts, wisteria
Nectar plants: Many garden and meadow flowers

Common Checkered Skipper *Pyrgus communis*

WINGSPAN AVERAGE
1" (25 MM)

BREEDING RANGE

While most Skippers are not considered attractive, the Common Checkered is quite nice. In fact, under some circumstances it can even be considered beautiful. Basic coloration can vary with this species, with the upper surface being charcoal gray to black with white checks merging to form dark bands. The fringe edging both wings is checkered in gray, white, and black. On the underside of the wings are wavy rows of tan, green, or white, but it's the body that makes this creature special: It's covered with hairlike scales that cast a beautiful bluish reflection in the sunlight.

Common Checkereds can be found nectaring from a large assortment of garden flowers, with their wings laid flat. If you happen on one of these delightful skippers, take the time to — ahem — check it out. Quite intricate, they are well worth the look.

Host plants: Hollyhock, hibiscus, wild mallows
Nectar plants: Many garden and meadow flowers

Look for the eggs on the leaves of mallows. They begin life green and change to a creamy color right before hatching.

The tan or brown caterpillars have a dark stripe down the back and brown and white side stripes running the length of the body. A coating of thick white hair covers the entire larva. Length: 1¼" (30 mm)

The chrysalis is most often green at the top and becomes brown toward the bottom.

Long-Tailed Skipper *Urbanus proteus*

BREEDING RANGE

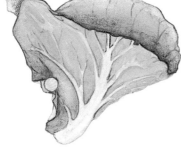

Look for the green, ribbed, globular-shaped eggs on leaves of plants in the bean and cabbage families.

The caterpillars appear as if they are sprinkled with yellow and black dots. Length: 1¼" (30 mm)

The chrysalis is less than an inch long, brown with a patina of yellow and blue, and quite reminiscent of abalone shell.

WINGSPAN AVERAGE 2" (50 MM)

Southern gardeners are well aware of the Bean Leaf Roller, since it is such an avid visitor to vegetable patches. This yellowish green caterpillar with the big brown head has been causing havoc below the Mason-Dixon line for quite some time. If it is allowed to mature, it will become the Long-Tailed Skipper.

Skippers don't normally win many beauty contests, but this one is interesting to look at. It definitely resembles a moth, or maybe a miniature bat with a touch of swallowtail thrown in for good measure. Best of all, the scales cast a wonderful iridescent blue halo across its body when the sunlight hits them just right.

The most noticeable points about this 2-inch-wide lep just may be its tail and fishhook-style antennae. On the forewings, from the center towards the tips, are white dashes, noticeable from underneath as well. The hind wings are somber brown with noticeable dark stripes showing on the underside.

Host plants: Beans and other legumes, crucifers, canna lilies
Nectar plants: Many garden and meadow flowers

NEOTROPICALS

Looking very tropical, the wonderful Heliconia are a delight to watch. Whether in a live exhibit or along the Gulf Coast, they are mesmerizing. The Zebra Longwing and Crimson Patch make up this family. The Crimson may be found only in very small sections of southern Texas, but the Zebra can stray quite a distance, reaching far north.

They are easily recognizable by their slow flight and long, narrow wings. The caterpillars eat passionflowers and the adults collect pollen from the blooms. It is this ability to gather and digest pollen that allows the Longwings to live longer than most other butterflies. The Zebra is said to be one of the smarter butterflies and capable of short-term training.

A very unique habit of the Zebra Longwing is that at night adults will sleep in a group. They will gather at dusk and roost collectively at the ends of branches. The next morning they disperse and go about their day.

In this gallery the Gulf Fritillary is grouped with the Zebra Longwing because it shares the latter's passion for passionflowers. If you are out looking for Zebra you will probably bump into the Gulf or Malachite. They are not Heliconia, although they share the same stamping grounds.

Longwings make wonderful indoor butterflies that can be reared all year long.

Zebra Longwing *Heliconius charitonius*

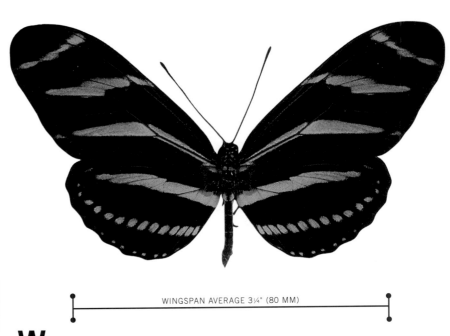

WINGSPAN AVERAGE 3¼" (80 MM)

BREEDING RANGE

Look for the yellow eggs of the Zebra on the tendrils of the passionflower.

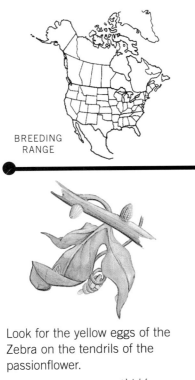

The black-spiked alabaster-white larva will become toxic from eating passionflower, making it an unpopular hors d'oeuvre among the local bird population. Length: 1½" (40 mm)

The thin, tan or brownish chrysalis has golden eyes and a long ornate horn protruding from the head.

With its long, black, yellow-striped wings, the Zebra looks as if it would be more at home in a tropical rain forest than in North America. When it's cruising and grooving, the slow beat of its wings seems barely enough to keep it in the air. Just try to catch it, however, and it's gone.

The Zebra Longwing is unusual in many ways. Considered one of the more intelligent leps, it's hard to confuse physically with any other. It's one of the few butterflies that can eat pollen, collecting it on its proboscis, then emitting a solution of enzymes and dining on the resulting liquid. This nutritous meal allows it to live longer than most butterflies. At night, Zebras prefer to sleep with others of their kind, and it's not unusual to find large numbers of them clinging to the tip of the same branch.

When a male is ready to mate, it will locate the chrysalis of a female and open it just enough to allow for mating to take place. Afterward, it deposits a small amount of pheromone to discourage any other suitors.

The Zebra chrysalis is just as fascinating as the other stages. When the thin, tan or brownish pupa is held upside down, it resembles an artist's concept of a miniature devil, with horns and glaring golden eyes, more than it does a butterfly chrysalis. With a long, ornate horn protruding from the head and golden eyes staring back, it is impressive and scary indeed.

The Zebra prefers the warmer climate of the southern tier of the United States, where it will have many broods, but natural dispersal causes it to venture northward from time to time. You will love the beauty of this insect and its fairylike flight pattern.

Host plants: Passionflower
Nectar plants: Hibiscus, pentas, lantana

Gulf Fritillary *Agraulis vanillae*

WING SPAN AVERAGE 4½–6" (100 MM)

BREEDING RANGE

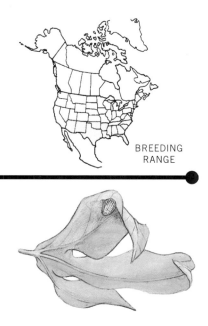

Look for the ribbed, oblong, yellow eggs only on passionflowers.

The black spiny caterpillars are lined with red and dotted with cream. The larvae ingest the toxin of their host plant, which renders them poisonous to predators. Length: 1½" (40 mm)

The long, narrow pupa is curved and can be brown or greenish brown with assorted patches of gray or brown. This gives it the appearance of a hanging leaf.

This fritillary doesn't fit the mold and seems more like a tropical species. Other Frits eat violets, but the Gulf prefers to dine on passionflowers. The orange and black markings on the upper surfaces of the wings seem consistent with the patterns of the other fritillaries. Underneath, however, the Gulf is a work of art, with a beautiful pattern of silver and red.

Favoring the southern tier and Gulf States, this butterfly still has no problem straying as far north as Minnesota. Unfortunately, it cannot survive freezing temperatures and perishes as winter arrives. However, passionflowers do well indoors and yield beautiful intricate blooms. The Gulf Fritillary also does well indoors and can live for quite a while. The combination of the two makes this lep a serious choice for rearing indoors during the long winter months.

Host plants: Passionflower

Nectar plants: Hibiscus, pentas, lantana

Malachite *Siproeta stelenes*

Look for the dark green egg on yerba papagayo. Usually a single egg is laid, though occasionally two or three eggs may be placed together.

The 2-inch larvae are black with purple or red between the segments. Two hornlike red projections curve back from the head, and the body is covered with red spines. Don't touch this caterpillar. Length: 2" (50 mm)

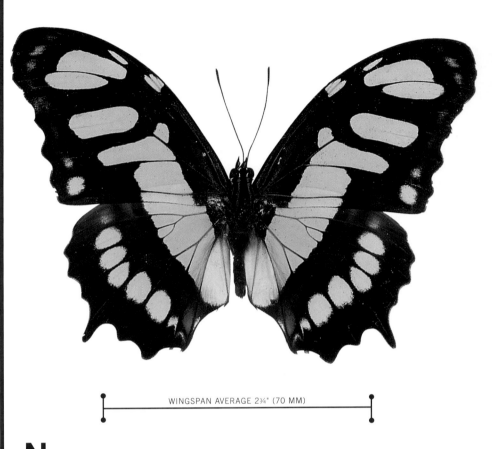

WINGSPAN AVERAGE 2¾" (70 MM)

Not everyone in North America will be able to see the Malachite, and that's a shame. Its unusual colors would cause most people to think a tropical stray had wandered by. From above, the ebony wings appear to be made of black velvet, inlaid with pieces of jade. The undersides of both the front and the back wings are green, highlighted with white, and nicely complemented by a border of tan along the outer margin. Found mostly in Florida and Texas, the Malachite has been known to stray as far as Kansas.

This impressive little wonder is a favorite in live exhibits, so if the opportunity presents itself, try to see it. If you come across a Malachite caterpillar, however, take heed. The spines of older larvae can induce a rash in some people. Furthermore, the caterpillar will release a green fluid if disturbed.

Host plants: Yerba papagayo and other related species
Adults prefer: Rotting fruit, dung, mud

The chrysalis is done up in the usual Art Deco colors: lime green trimmed in pink dots.

ODDITIES

The Harvester and the Snout are butterflies unto themselves, with only one representative of each living in North America. After reading about all the other larger families, we should almost feel sorry for these lonely two. The Harvester belongs to the Gossamer Wings, while the Snout belongs to the Libytheidae (lib-i-THEE-ah-dee) family, which is the smallest of all the butterfly families in North America.

The adult Harvester very rarely visits flowers, preferring to gather honeydew from the aphids it grew up among.

Harvester *Feniseca tarquinius*

BREEDING
RANGE

Look for the eggs, which are greenish-tinted white and lightly grooved, right in the middle of a population of woolly aphids on leaves of alder and other shrubs.

The greenish brown caterpillar is carnivorous and feeds only on woolly aphids. It buries itself in debris before pupating. Length: ½" (10 mm)

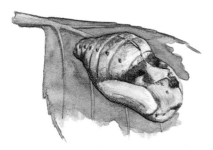

The brown pupa resembles a monkey's face.

WINGSPAN AVERAGE
1¼" (30 MM)

Small and unattractive could best describe the Harvester. However, fascinating and amazing would work just as well. The Harvester may not catch your eye, but it is worthy of attention because of its unusual habits. It's hard to believe that this small brown and orange butterfly is actually, in its caterpillar stage, a devious, Gossamer Wing insectivore.

Oddly enough, Harvester eggs are not deposited on a host plant; rather, they are placed singly into a colony of aphids, the larvae's favorite food. The Harvester caterpillar's life revolves around aphids, which it eats. Aphids secrete a "honeydew" liquid from the excess fluids that they suck from plants like alder, beech, and witch hazel. This sweet delicacy is prized by ants, who in exchange offer the aphids protection from such predators as Harvester caterpillars.

To avoid detection, the caterpillar covers itself with a loose webbing, made of bits of aphid skins, honeydew, and droppings. Once it has emerged into an adult, the Harvester will still prefer sipping nectar from aphids rather than visiting flowers.

Host plants: Caterpillars feed exclusively on woolly aphids living on alders, witch hazel, ash, beech, hawthorn, and wild currant.

Nectar plants: Adults do not nectar but stay near populations of aphids to consume honeydew.

American Snout *Libytheana bachmanii*

WINGSPAN AVERAGE 1¾" (45 MM)

Look for the tiny brown eggs of the Snout butterfly on hackberry.

The green caterpillars have yellow stripes and a fondness for hackberry. Length: 1¼" (30 mm)

The chrysalis is pointed and ridged.

These butterflies are called Snouts because the two species that inhabit the United States are named for their overdeveloped palpi, which look like big old snouts. These rusty orange-and-black aeronauts are capable of great emigrations and can be found far from their homes. On its home turf, the American Snout can be found east of the Rockies, while the Southern Snout prefers Arizona and Texas, with an occasional vacation northward.

Host plant: Hackberry
Nectar plants: Rabbitbrush, dogwood, peach

Taking the Plunge!

Year-Round Fun-with-Butterfly Activities

Think of the enjoyment you've gotten from raising butterflies, the awe of watching an adult emerge from its chrysalis. Maybe it's time to help others realize this same pleasure. Or maybe you're at the point where you feel that you have too many butterflies for your own good (if that could ever really be a problem). No matter what the reason, you should consider participating in activities that will take your avocation to the next level of "butterflydom" — activities that will not only take you deeper within the world of butterflies, but ones that can also help you raise public awareness about them and their plight. Not only that, you can also help unravel many of the mysteries that still surround these magnificent creatures.

It's a sunny day, and the meadow is calling.

RED ADMIRAL CHRYSALIS

Share the Joy

By this time you've raised some butterflies and increased your lepidopteran knowledge. And you're probably even feeling better as a result. The soothing, Zenlike aspect of living with butterflies naturally calms you down. You're no doubt noticing plants now as you never have before. You've probably even developed a better appreciation of *all* living things. Now it's time to open your newly discovered world to your friends, and sharing is always an added bonus when butterflies are involved.

Metamorphoses

Want to make your friends really happy? Give them a chrysalis. They'll thank you for years to come. People just don't forget the time that "their" butterfly was born. No matter who they are — construction workers, students, lawyers — *everyone,* no matter how seemingly tough, marvels at the beauty of a newly emerged butterfly.

Turnaround

For some years I had the pleasure of teaching a program for Rutgers University in New Jersey. Under the aegis of the New Jersey Department of Corrections, the Green Industry Program was presented to youthful offenders and kids at risk to show them that it was possible to work constructively with animals for commercial gain. Well, talk about metamorphosis. These mostly streetwise, inner-city kids had never been exposed to wildlife in a natural setting. But when given the chance to raise butterflies and plants in a greenhouse atmosphere, they themselves transformed into some very impressive individuals. Kids who had grown up way too fast, seen way more in life than they should have, with no chance to stop and watch the butterflies, were suddenly allowed to experience a carefree childhood. And the transformation was nothing short of astonishing. The look of inquisitive wonderment in their eyes as they fed "their" personal butterflies can't be described. Nor can I describe how good their hugs and soul-piercing thank yous felt as they finished their courses. The best times were always when they were given nets and allowed to careen madly around the facility's grounds to catch whatever they could: laughter to the point of pain, good-natured frustration over fleeing quarry, cheerful embarrassment over missing an easy shot in front of peers, fresh air, and healthy exercise. After every outing I was always told, "Thanks, man, that was the most fun I ever had." After six years of being allowed this opportunity, I now firmly believe that just about anyone can be reached through butterflies. So it's important to share this information.

ZEBRA SWALLOWTAIL

Living Gifts

One of the nicest things you can do is to give a chrysalis to someone who is ill. On several occasions I have received heartfelt thank you letters from people who had just returned home after a hospital stay. During that time, they were sent a hatching kit fashioned from an ice-cream sundae dish (see chapter 3). After watching their "baby" struggle to emerge, dry its wings, and take to the sky with their wish, their private battles seemed a bit more tolerable. And, of course, the self-contained hatching kit is clean and safe with no muss or fuss.

Since nothing can compare to the joy of watching a child watching a butterfly, if you have a few extra leps, donate them to your child's school. If you don't have children, then adopt a school. The kids will love you for it. Explain the proper use of the various rearing containers mentioned in this book. Explain to them how important it is to recycle and to grow before you throw. You'll be teaching two important lessons, and helping both butterflies and children in the process.

Children of all ages love to watch butterflies eat.

Children, no matter what age, love to watch animals eat, and butterflies are no exception. So show them how it's done. A little sugar water on the end of a cotton swab and voila! Instant captivation. Not only will the kids be totally fascinated and think that you're a genius, they will never look at butterflies the same way again. Why, they may even buy and plant some of those flowers you told them about. The end result is that they became aware — and butterflies benefit.

Nursing homes and assisted-care facilities are great places to share your devotion with potential friends who would crave such pleasure. For most residents, many years have passed since they last chased butterflies through their gardens. I guarantee that if you take butterflies to them, you will be rewarded with some tears of joy as memories of long-ago warm summer days wash over them. Most of us have been told almost from birth not to touch a butterfly, so being finally allowed to do so somehow makes life — even near its end — fuller. For a few moments, an ailing elder will metamorphose into a smiling child, and the world becomes a better place, if only for a little while. So if you have a few extra leps, make a hanging cage for your spares, and present them to a nursing home. You will touch many lives — but mostly your own.

Collecting Farther Afield

Now that you're comfortable and confident with your garden residents, you may decide to branch out a bit by trying to rear species not found in your backyard. Collecting may be a good way to introduce new bloodlines into your breeding stock. But much care needs to be taken, and a number of issues need to be addressed. The first is where you plan your excursion and forays. Always ask permission to tread on private land. Not only would the owners appreciate this common courtesy, it may also save you from getting a load of buckshot in the backside rather than a Buckeye in the bag.

During the winter months you can more easily spot a chrysalis or cocoon against bare branches.

Also, keep in mind that it's illegal to collect in national or state parks. In some parks even the sight of a net will be cause to search your car. It may sound drastic, but it's necessary for the welfare of the wildlife in the parks. If someone were to invade a park and remove all the leps, none would be left for others to enjoy. There are plenty of other public and private places to utilize for your collecting safaris, so when visiting a park, use only a camera.

Parks are often unique areas with equally unique wildlife. This makes the localized lep population special, often because they are endangered or rare. Unfortunately, this places a high value on them for some unscrupulous people devoid of environmental consciousness. A thriving black market exists everywhere, and the illegal trade of butterflies will testify to this. In fact, one group of poachers openly bragged about dealing only in endangered species acquired illegally from national parks. Thankfully, for publicly flaunting their escapades, the group will only be reading about butterflies for five to fifteen years — at the Leavenworth prison library.

Seasonal Collecting

Autumn and winter collecting is always a fun-time family activity. When the leaves have fallen from the trees, chrysalises and cocoons will be revealed. Many moth cocoons quite visibly hang from branches during the winter months, looking like rolled up chambers of leaves. Logically, the larger a cocoon is, the larger the emerging moth will be. Chrysalises, on the other hand, are usually smoother and less conspicuous. They can be found underneath loose bark on trees, beneath fallen logs, or attached to branches. Overwintering chrysalises are usually camouflaged rather well. That's their job, to hide until spring. With a little practice, locating them gets easier. Why, before you know it, you'll be noticing them while cruising down the highway at the posted speed limit.

Look before You Lep

Our lives are busy today, and things need to get done in a hurry. Perhaps you don't have time to plant a garden or go out collecting in your woods. After doing some extra reading or Internet surfing, you've no doubt discovered that many suppliers out there offer various live specimens. Two words of advice: Be careful.

Most dealers are reputable, but there are renegades in any walk of life, and butterfly collecting is no exception. Before you purchase live butterflies from outside your state, be advised: *It's illegal to take a live butterfly across a state line!* Sure, Monarchs fly back and forth between Canada and Mexico during migration, crossing both state and international boundaries in the process. Yes, those Painted Ladies emigrate to wherever they please. *But you can't help them to do it.* Not without strict approval, anyway.

For any living butterfly to legally cross a state line on anything other than its own power, it must be accompanied by a USDA-approved PPQ 526 permit. This seemingly harsh regulation is actually much needed for the welfare of agriculture in general. The permits are designed to curb such fiascos as the artificial (as opposed to natural) introduction of Gypsy Moths and the notorious Cabbage White butterfly into new environments. Gypsy Moths were intentionally released after they were found unfit for their intended application of replacing silkworms. And after being brought in from Europe, the Cabbage White, which is probably the most familiar butterfly on the continent, escaped from its temporary home in Canada in 1890 and can now be found everywhere in North America, happily dining on garden vegetables.

If you are determined to acquire some out-of-state leps, you must get a legal permit — unless you have a taste for prison food or have large sums of money to throw away on fines. You can now file for the PPQ 526 permits electronically on the Internet, but it can take a few weeks, or in some cases a few months, before they're approved. (A sample permit is shown in the Appendix.) To start, check with your state's Department of Agriculture; the number is usually listed in the blue pages of your phone book.

A Stiff Penalty

After President Clinton signed the Plant Protection Act, a $50,000 fine was imposed for illegally transporting butterflies.

Native Is Best

Even though some leps are seemingly everywhere, they are still protected. You can't use the argument that since there are lots of them in, say, California, why not bring in a few to release in your garden in St. Louis. It may not be good for the butterfly or for the native vegetation. A worst-case scenario would be someone living in an orange-producing state acquiring citrus-eating butterflies and having them escape. It could be disastrous to local farmers. It would be equally unfair to release a butterfly in an area where it could not possibly survive. You may profess, "But I'll have it in captivity just until I take some pictures." That's no doubt just what was said prior to the exodus of Cabbage White. It's just not worth the chance environmentally.

A Butterfly in Winter

If you do pursue the permit process, you could benefit by raising butterflies throughout the winter. Some species, such as the Zebra Longwing and the Gulf Fritillary, do very well indoors. Both consume the passionflower, a very beautiful and exotic-looking plant that produces exquisite blooms and also does well indoors. Complemented with a pentas or two for nectar, your Zebras and Gulfs will be quite happy spending the holidays at your home.

Living Ornaments

You might wonder: What happens when you then have dozens of butterflies flapping all around your house? The answer is: You are stuck in heaven. Butterflies will usually gravitate toward light coming in through the window curtains, where they can be easily caught and placed inside the hanging cages described on page 52. With the proper plants, they would prefer to linger there rather than to roam through your house.

Ambient room temperature, humidity, and some extra lighting is often all that's needed to raise butterflies during the colder months. By rearing just a few, not much space is required, and as for extra light, a sunny window or perhaps a shop light above a table is often just enough. If you keep it small, it'll be very manageable. One butterfly born on Christmas morning is every bit as magical as a hundred being born. Wouldn't you just love to sit back on a freezing cold day and look out over 12 inches of newly fallen snow as Lloyd, your pet Zebra Longwing, gently glissades across the living room?

RICK'S TIPS

Butterflies can't be released if the temperature is below 60°F, because they physically cannot fly. You should never release non-natives into any area, since they will not find their host plants and will die. It's also illegal. Only certain species can be released anywhere in the United States.

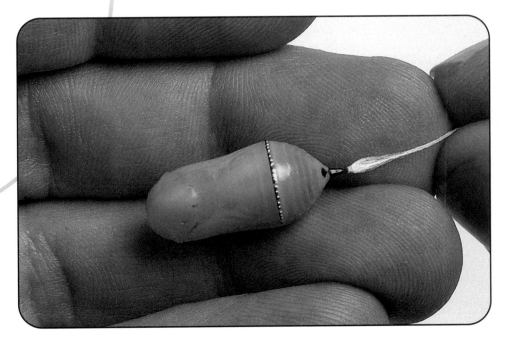

One of our favorite things to do is to time the emergence of our butterflies to Christmas Day. A week or two before Christmas, our family fashions Christmas tree decorations using chrysalises. The silk of the chrysalis is tied around ornament hooks and then hung from the tree. With the proper room temperature and a bit of misting from a water bottle, the butterflies burst forth from their resting places and spread their wings on Christmas morning.

Photography Tips and Tricks

It isn't necessary to collect, kill, and pin butterflies in order to enjoy them. Sure, scientific or educational institutions require extensive collections, but photographing them is the perfect alternative for the rest of us.

And photographs are another wonderful way to share butterflies with others. After all, you put in all that time and trouble to raise them, so surely you're entitled to take some baby pictures. Besides, if you ever decide to enter a photography contest, you'll be far ahead of the pack with a good butterfly picture. Butterflies instantly capture the eye, and everyone is intrigued by them. So start shooting.

Necessary Equipment

Personally, I quit trying to keep abreast of all the latest photography breakthroughs years ago. If you read photography magazines and Web sites, you'll quickly discover that the newest and the best equipment is incredibly expensive. Instead of spending a fortune, use a bit of thought and common sense. I still get my best shots from a 25-year-old $150 Minolta X-G7 body and a $99 zoom lens. The lens is variable from 80 mm to 210 mm, with a minimum focal distance of 6 feet. In the field you'd be very lucky to get much closer than 6 feet from a butterfly before it will flee. With the zoom at its maximum, the frame will be filled with the creature. If the shot turns out to be a keeper, it can be blown up to any size desired.

Here are some other tools and tricks of the trade.

Diopter Lenses

If you have a standard 35 mm camera, it's easy and inexpensive to take your shooting ability up a notch by using a diopter lens set. These close-up lenses screw onto your existing camera lens like a filter and are available in different powers: +1, +2, and +3. Each lens is good for a certain range of distances. The higher the number, the more powerful the lens, and the closer you can get to your subject. In fact, these lenses will allow you to get within inches, if not one inch, from your subject. You can use diopter lenses in combinations to get even closer to your subject. For example, a +1 lens and a +3 lens equals a +4 lens. Whichever combination you choose, always use the strongest diopter lens next to the camera lens. A set of diopter close-up lenses costs around $30.

Tubes, Converters, and Rings

Extension tubes will also get you close-up pictures without having to spend a fortune on a macro lens. Extension tubes are hollow metal tubes that fit between the camera and the lens. They are normally sold in sets of three, like the diopter lenses. If you were to add, say, a 25 mm extension tube to your 50 mm macro lens, you could take a twice-life-sized picture. Extension tubes will cost you from $50 to $150.

Another way is to use a teleconverter. They are more expensive than extension tubes because they have optics, but they are more versatile. A 2X converter will give a 50 mm lens the power of a 100 mm lens, a 3X will give you 150 mm, and so forth. You can expect to pay in the neighborhood of $200 for a teleconverter.

There is also the option of using reversing rings, which attach a lens backward to the camera body, effectively turning it into a close-up lens. The average cost of reversing rings is $20 to $30.

Just remember, though, that a butterfly isn't going to wait for you to screw on rings, teleconverters, or extension tubes. You'll have to grab the shot when you can.

Macro/Micro Lenses

These are typically available in lengths of 50 mm and 100 mm; the longer focal length allows you to focus on small subjects from farther away. Macro lenses are convenient because you can use them for close-ups for one photo and then for a distant shot for the next. You don't have the hassle of coupling or disconnecting setups or searching in your camera bag for missing parts. But you'd better be prepared to spend for one of these puppies because they can range from around $200 to thousands of dollars. Still, they are well worth the money and will probably be the last lens that you'll feel you "need" to buy.

Point and Shoots

Many of the new point-and-shoot cameras have a macro setting that allows you to get within six inches of the subject. (Any closer than that and you'd crush the poor little thing.) Many of the point-and-shoots fall in the $99 to $150 price range and have everything you could want: red-eye reduction, macro, built-in flash, auto film loading, and film dedication all in one package. Small, compact, and reliable, they fit into a pocket for quick retrieval when the situation arises.

Digitals

Some new digital cameras sell for less than $100. They have everything the 35-mm SLRs have, plus they can be downloaded right into your computer. And, since they're digital, you'll never run out of film again. The best part: Once loaded onto your hard drive, your shots can be manipulated, warped, and recolored at whim.

Rare Photos

Some rare species of butterflies have never been photographed, even in their adult form. For many species, there are no photographs of eggs, caterpillars, or chrysalises.

Digital cameras offer macro, flash, zoom, auto focus, and every bell and whistle that's available with any other type of camera. Of course, you will pay for these extras (sometimes many hundreds of dollars) but think what you'll save in film!

When investigating digital cameras, focus — so to speak — on the image sharpness and resolution. The quality of the end picture is determined by the pixel count. Anything between 640 x 480 and 1280 x 1024 is good. Digital cameras are just like your computer: They work on memory. The more memory, the more images that can be stored in the camera. Called *flash memory,* anywhere from one to two megs is standard. There is no end to the creative things you can do with a digital camera. All types of special software and papers are available for your color printer to make your photos into greeting cards and calendars, or just to embarrass your family and friends in cyberspace.

The real beauty of digital cameras is how easily corrections can be made on your computer. You never need to worry about film speed, available light, f-stops, or any other headaches, as you would with conventional photography. You can remove dust and scratches and red eye, or you can make night look like day. If you're thinking about buying a camera, you may be better off choosing a digital one. It's just so much more flexible than standard 35-mm photography.

Other Photo Tips

Odd though it may seem, one of the most important pieces of equipment in your photographic quest is your refrigerator. Why? Because if you want to get great pictures, cool your subject down. Butterflies are warm blooded. Place one in the fridge in any type of container or the envelope described in the Appendix for 5 minutes — no more than that — and the lep will quickly fall asleep. When it's reintroduced to room temperature, it will slowly begin to wake up. Before it does so completely, you'll have a window of opportunity to grab some great shots.

Butterflies warm themselves by flapping their wings — slowly at first, and then, as the internal temperature rises, faster. Once the proper temperature is achieved, they will fly off. You'll quickly develop a talent for shooting while the wings are open and advancing the film when they're closed. This is the perfect setup for, say, photographing butterflies on people's noses. Remove the butterfly from the fridge and place it onto your subject's nose . . . perhaps he or she can pretend to be asleep. Shoot like crazy, and get ready to add another award to your photo gallery. This technique also works well for videotaping. The procedure is followed as described above. Then, by reversing the film, it will look as if the butterfly came to rest on the subject, not as if it was flying away.

The refrigeration method will also work to capture the moment a butterfly emerges from a chrysalis. Very close to the point of emergence, chrysalises become the color of the butterfly inside. Actually, what you see is the butterfly showing through the almost transparent pupal case. At that point, they can be placed in the fridge to stop development while you set up your shot. Arrange your background and lighting, remove the chrysalis, and place it in the shot. It should emerge within an hour, and you'll have some pretty impressive pictures. Just remember this simple rule: Cooler temperatures slow things down, and warmer temperatures speed them up.

A drop of sugar water on your model's nose may persuade a butterfly to linger long enough to be photographed.

ZEBRA LONGWING

Conclusion

Most people involved with butterflies are so because, in some way or another, these creatures touched their lives.

A woman once told me the story of how she and her father had always shared the delight of butterflies. While she was growing up, they would often venture into the nearby fields and enjoy what they found there. When, years later, her father's health began to fade, they would look out over the garden just to watch butterflies, or they'd read about them in books and magazines. He eventually passed away, and at his funeral she sat in the front pew to lovingly say good-bye to her best friend. When the service began, a butterfly flew into the church, landed on her hand, and stayed there for the entire time. At the conclusion of the service, after spending a last few moments with her, the butterfly flew out of the church. How could anyone possibly argue that it was not her father reassuring her that he would never be far away?

So be a friend to butterflies, and butterflies will never be far away from you.

Off to seek its fortune, this Monarch butterfly could travel several thousand miles in its lifetime.

HARDINESS ZONES FOR COMMON HOST PLANTS

Anise *(Pimpinella anisum)* Hardy annual

Ash *(Fraxinus)* Zones 3 to 9

Aspen *(Populus tremuloides)* Zones 2 to 9

Aster *(Aster)* Zones 3 to 8

Bee balm/bergamot *(Monarda)* Zones 4 to 9

Bleeding heart *(Dicentra* spp.) Zone 11

Blueberry *(Vaccinium)* Zones 3 to 9

Bottlebrush *(Callistemon)* Zones 8 to 10

Buckthorn *(Rhamnus)* Zones 3 to 9

Butterfly bush *(Buddleia davidii)* Zones 5 to 9

Butterfly weed *(Asclepias tuberosa)* Zones 4 to 9

Buttonbush *(Cephalanthus occidentalis)* Zones 5 to 11

Cabbage *(Brassica oleracea* Capitata Group) Hardy biennial

Calico pipe *(Aristolochia littoralis)* Zones 10 to 11

Carrot *(Daucus carota)* Hardy biennial

Caryopteris *(Caryopteris)* Zones 7 to 9

Cherry *(Prunus)* Zones 4 to 9

Chokecherry *(Prunus virginiana)* Zones 3 to 8

Citrus *(Citrus)* Zones 9 to 11

Clover, white or red *(Trifolium)* Zones 5 to 9

Common stock *(Matthiola incana)* Zones 7 to 8

Crown flower *(Calitropis gigantius)* Zone 11

Dill *(Anethum graveolens)* Hardy annual

Dogwood *(Cornus* spp.) Zones 5 to 9

Dutchman's-pipe *(Aristolochia durior)* Zones 4 to 8

Elm *(Ulmus)* Zones 3 to 9

Eucalyptus *(Eucalyptus)* Zones 9 to 11

False indigo *(Amorpha)* Zones 2 to 7

Fennel *(Foeniculum vulgare)* Zones 5 to 11

Hackberry *(Celtis occidentalis)* Zones 2 to 9

Hollyhock *(Alcea rosea)* Zones 4 to 8

Hop *(Humulus)* Zones 4 to 8

Koa *(Acacia koa)* Zones 10 to 11

Lantana *(Lantana camara)* Zones 9 to 11

Lavender *(Lavendula)* Zones 5 to 7

Lilac *(Syringa)* Zones 3 to 7

Live oak *(Quercus virginiana)* Zones 8 to 10

Lupine *(Lupinus)* Zones 3 to 8

Mallow *(Malva)* Zones 4 to 8

Marigold *(Tagetes)* Tender annual

Milkweed *(Asclepias)* Zones 3 to 9

Mint *(Mentha)* Zones 5 to 9

Mustard *(Brassica)* Hardy annual

Nasturtium *(Tropaeolum)* Hardy annual

Nettle *(Urtica)* Zones 5 to 9

Oak *(Quercus)* Zones 2 to 11

Parsley *(Petroselinum crispum)* Hardy biennial

Passionflower *(Passiflora)* Zone 10

Pea *(Pisum sativum)* Hardy annual

Phlox *(Phlox)* Zones 3 to 9

Poplar *(Populus)* Zones 3 to 9

Queen Anne's lace *(Daucus carota)* Hardy biennial

Sassafras *(Sassafras albidum)* Zones 5 to 8

Snapdragon *(Antirrhinum majus)* Tender perennial

Spicebush *(Lindera benzoin)* Zones 5 to 9

Stonecrop *(Sedum)* Zones 3 to 8

Sunflower *(Helianthus annuus)* Tender annual

Sweet bay *(Magnolia virginiana)* Zones 6 to 9

Sweet William *(Dianthus barbatus)* Hardy biennial

Thistle *(Cirsium)* Zones 5 to 7

Tickseed *(Coreopsis)* Zones 4 to 9

Tulip tree *(Liriodendron tulipifera)* Zones 4 to 9

Verbena *(Verbena)* Tender annual

Vetch *(Hippocrepis)* Zones 5 to 7

Violet *(Viola)* Zones 5 to 8

Virginia snakeroot *(Aristolochia serpentaria)* Zones 5 to 9

Wild cherry *(Prunus serotina)* Zones 4 to 8

Wild lime *(Zanthoxylum fagara)* Zones 6 to 9

Willow *(Salix)* Zones 2 to 8

Yarrow *(Achillea millefolium)* Zones 3 to 8

USDA HARDINESS ZONE MAP

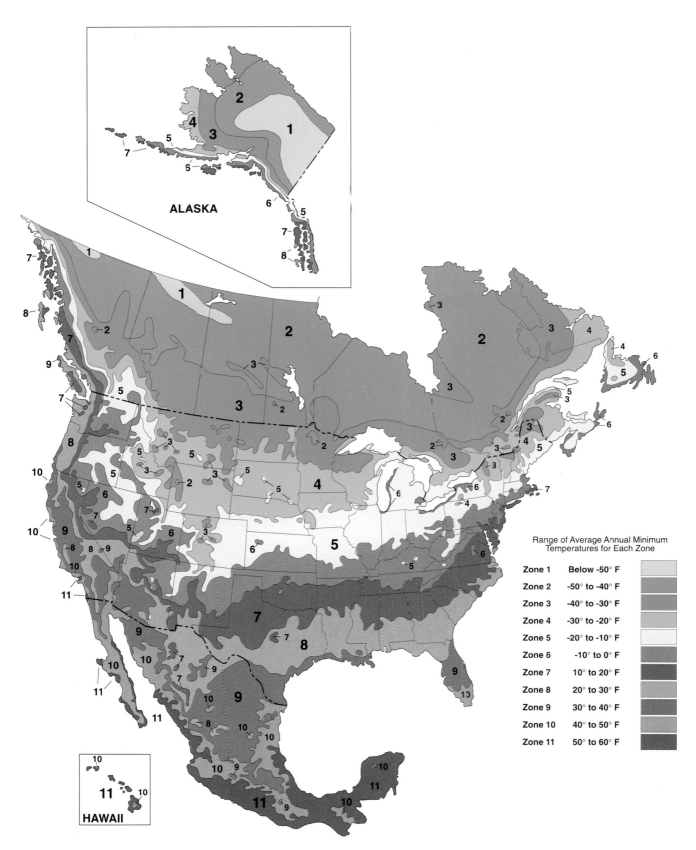

ALASKA

HAWAII

Range of Average Annual Minimum
Temperatures for Each Zone

Zone 1	Below -50° F
Zone 2	-50° to -40° F
Zone 3	-40° to -30° F
Zone 4	-30° to -20° F
Zone 5	-20° to -10° F
Zone 6	-10° to 0° F
Zone 7	10° to 20° F
Zone 8	20° to 30° F
Zone 9	30° to 40° F
Zone 10	40° to 50° F
Zone 11	50° to 60° F

Make a Butterfly Envelope

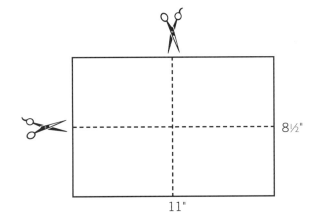

8½"

11"

You can transport butterflies in these easy-to-make envelopes. All you need is a sheet of regular 8½" x 11" paper, cut into four equal pieces, as indicated in the sketch at left.

1. Fold the small rectangular section on the diagonal to form two overlapping triangles.

2. Place the butterfly, with its wings folded together, inside the folded paper. Turn the butterfly upside down, if necessary, to calm it.

3. Fold the flaps in opposite directions to seal the envelope, and "lock" it by twisting the small end flaps.

4. Keep the butterfly envelope in a cool, dim place until it's time for release.

DEVELOPMENT TIME FOR SELECTED BUTTERFLY SPECIES

These are generalized guidelines for species that would be easiest to find in a garden setting. The values calculated in this chart are for an average daytime temperature of 75 – 80°F with approximately 70–80% humidity. Light, temperature, and humidity can lengthen or shorten timing considerably. Latitude and time of year can also cause great variations, as will the availability of food. In the northern ranges, most butterflies will overwinter in the chrysalis stage, but some will use the larval or egg stage. Naturally, there will be more broods, or generations, in southern areas than in the cooler north.

SPECIES	LARVAE FOOD	EGG COLOR	DAYS AS EGG	DAYS AS LARVA	DAYS AS PUPA	BROOD
American Copper	Sorrel	Green	4	14	10	4
American Painted Lady	Everlasting	Yellowish green	3–5	10–14	7–10	2
Painted Lady	Mallows and thistles	Green	4–5	7–14	7–10	2–3
Baltimore Checkerspot*	Turtlehead	Yellow-orange	21	10–14	10	1
Buckeye*	Plantain	Green	5	14	10–12	2
Cabbage White	Cabbage and nasturtiums	Yellow-white	5	14	10	3–5
Clouded Sulphur	Clover and alfalfa	White	5–6	21	10	3–4
Black Swallowtail	Parsley and carrots	Yellow-white	5	10–14	12	2–3
Spicebush Swallowtail	Spicebush and sassafras	Yellow-white	5–7	14–21	14	2–3
Eastern Tiger Swallowtail	Cherry and willow	Yellow-white	5–7	14–21	14	2–3
Giant Swallowtail	Citrus	Yellow	4–5	12–14	10–14	2
Question Mark**	Hops and nettles	Green	5–7	21	10–14	2
Green Comma**	Nettles and elm	Green	5–7	21	10–14	2
Mourning Cloak**	Willow and poplar	Yellow-brown	10–12	14	8–12	2–3
Red Admiral	Nettles	Green	4–5	14	7–10	2–3
Viceroy	Willow and cherry	Brown	4–5	14–18	7–10	2
Great Spangled Fritillary*	Violets	Yellow-white	3–4	14; hibernates	9–18	1–2
Snout	Hackberry	Green	4	30	21	2
Monarch***	Milkweed	Ivory	3–5	10–14	10–14	3
Zebra Longwing	Passiflora	Golden yellow	5–6	10–14	8–12	2–3
Gulf Fritillary	Passiflora	Yellow	5	10	7–10	2–3
Harvester	Woolly aphids	Greenish white	3–4	8–10	8–12	2–3
Silver-Spotted Skipper	Locust and legumes	Green with red tip	4	14	14	1–3
Red-Spotted Purple*	Willow and cherry	Grayish green	5	14–18	7–10	1–3
Pearly Crescentspot*	Asters	Pale green	4–6	10–12	7–12	3–4

* Species that overwinters as caterpillars
** Species that overwinters as adults
*** Species that overwinters in Mexico

USDA PERMIT TO TRANSPORT BUTTERFLIES ACROSS STATE LINES

No permit can be issued to move live plant pests or noxiuos weeds until an application is received (7 CFR 330 (live plant pests) or 7 CFR 360 (noxious weeds))

See reverse side for additional OMB information.

FORM APPROVED
OMB NO. 0579-0054

U.S DEPARTMENT OF AGRICULTURE
ANIMAL AND PLANT HEALTH INSPECTION SERVICE
PLANT PROTECTION AND QUARANTINE
BIOLOGICAL ASSESSMENT AND TAXONOMIC SUPPORT
RIVERDALE, MARYLAND 20737

APPLICATION AND PERMIT TO MOVE
LIVE PLANT PESTS OR NOXIOUS WEEDS

SECTION A - TO BE COMPLETED BY THE APPLICANT

1. NAME, TITLE, AND ADDRESS *(Include Zip Code)*

3. TYPE OF PEST TO BE MOVED

* ☐ Pathogens ☐ Arthropods ☐ Noxious Weeds

☐ Other (Specify): _____

This permit does not authorize the introduction, importation, interstate movement, or release into the environment of any genetically engineered organisms or products.

2. TELEPHONE NO. (   )

A. SCIENTIFIC NAMES OF PESTS TO BE MOVED	B. CLASSIFICATION (Orders, Families, Races, or Strains)	C. LIFE STAGES IF APPLI- CABLE	D. NO. OF SPECIMENS OR UNITS	E. SHIPPED FROM (Country or State)	F. ARE PESTS ESTABLISHED IN U.S.	G. MAJOR HOST(S) OF THE PEST
4.						
5.						
6.						

7. WHAT HOST MATERIAL OR SUBSTITUTES WILL ACCOMPANY WHICH PESTS *(Indicate by line number)*

8. DESTINATION

9. PORT OF ARRIVAL

10. APPROXIMATE DATE OF ARRIVAL OR INTERSTATE MOVEMENT

11. NO. OF SHIPMENTS

12. SUPPLIER

13. METHOD OF SHIPMENT
☐ Air Mail ☐ Air Freight ☐ Baggage ☐ Auto

14. INTENDED USE **(Be specific, attach outline of intended research)**

15. METHODS TO BE USED TO PREVENT PLANT PEST ESCAPE

16. METHOD OF FINAL DISPOSITION

17. Applicant must be a resident of the U.S.A. I/We agree to comply with the safeguards printed on the reverse of this form, and understand that a permit may be subject to other conditions specified in Sections B and C.

SIGNATURE OF APPLICANT *(Must be person named in Item 1)*

18. DATE

SECTION B - TO BE COMPLETED BY STATE OFFICIAL

19. RECOMMENDATION

☐ Concur (Approve) ☐ Comments (Disapprove)

☐ (Accept USDA Decision)

20. CONDITIONS RECOMMENDED

21. SIGNATURE AND TITLE

22. TITLE

23. STATE

24. DATE

SECTION C - TO BE COMPLETED BY FEDERAL OFFICIAL

25. PERMIT NO.

PERMIT

(Permit not valid unless signed by an authorized official of the Animal and Plant Health Inspection Service)

Under authority of the Federal Plant Pest Act of May 23, 1957 or the Federal Noxious Weed Act of 1974, permission is hereby granted to the applicant named above to move the pests described, except as deleted, subject to the conditions stated on, or attached to this application. (See standard conditions on reverse side).

*For exotic plant pathogens, attach a completed PPQ form 526-1.

24. SIGNATURE OF PLANT PROTECTION AND QUARANTINE OFFICIAL	25. DATE	26. LABELS ISSUED	27. VALID UNTIL	28. PEST CATEGORY

CATCH BUTTERFLIES *ON* THE NET, NOT *WITH* ONE!

How to Contact the Author

The Butterfly Web Site
butterflywebsite.com

E-Page for this Book
butterflywebsite.com/thefamilybutterfly-book

Rick Mikula
holeinhand.com

Important Organizations

The International Butterfly Breeders Association
www.butterflybreeders.org
Attn: Chris Morigi
9148 Vanalden Street
Northridge, CA 91324

International Federation of Butterfly Enthusiasts (IFBE)
www.ifbe.org
109 Sundown Court
Chehalia, WA 98532

The Lepidopterists' Society
www.furman.edu/~snyder/snyder/lep
1900 John Street
Manhattan Beach, CA 90266-2608

Monarch Watch
www.monarchwatch.org
c/o O.R. Taylor, Dept. of Entomology
7005 Haworth Hall
University of Kansas
Lawrence, KS 66045
monarch@ukans.edu
Phone: 888-TAGGING
  or 785-864-4441
Fax: 785-864-4441
  or 785-864-5321

North American Butterfly Association
www.naba.org
4 Delaware Road
Morristown, NJ 07960

The Xerces Society
www.xerces.org
4828 SE Hawthorne Boulevard
Portland, OR 97215
Phone: 503-232-6639

Useful Web Sites

Backyard Wildlife Habitat project
www.nwf.org/habitats/index.html

The Butterfly Zone
www.butterflies.com

Children's butterfly sites
www.mesc.nbs.gov/butterfly/butterfly.html
www.mesc.usgs.gov/butterfly/butterfly-hotlist.html

Edible insects
www.eatbug.com
www.uky.edu/agriculture/entomology/yth-facts/bugfood/bugfood1.htm

Educational science
www.educationalscience.com
www.milkweedplants.com

Educators' recommended sites
Iowa State Entomology Index: K-12
www.ent.iastate.edu/list/k-12_educator_resources.html

Host plants database
www.nhm.ac.uk/entomology/hostplants/hostplant_search.html

Insect records
www.ifas.ufl.edu/~tjw/recbk.htm

Insectclopedia
www3.sympatico.ca/pedagonet

Journey North Migration
www.learner.org/jnorth

Let's Get Growing
www.letsgetgrowing.com

List of societies
www.ent.iastate.edu/list/societies.-html

National Wildlife Federation
www.nwf.org
8925 Leesburg Pike
Vienna, VA 22184
Phone: 703-790-4000

Perennials
www.ces.ncsu.edu/depts/hort/consumer/perennials

Stewardship projects
www.nwf.org/wildlifeweek/stewards.html

Teachers, young people, and anyone else who wants to pursue an interest in entomology
www.uky.edu/agriculture/entomology/yth-facts/entyouth.htm
www.isis.vt.edu

INDEX

Note: A **boldface** number indicates that a complete species description appears on that page.

I

Identification. See also specific butterflies
    by antennae, 11
    basics of, 91
Impatiens, 21, 31
Inbreeding, 79
Indigo, false, 26, 129
Indoors, raising butterflies, 150
Insecticides, 12, 13, 69, 79
Insects, other, 70, 73, 83, 94, 119,
    141–142
Instar, 6, 46

J

Jacob's ladder, 27
Jewelweed, 98
Joe-Pye weed, 25, 98
Julia, 81
Junonia coenia. See Buckeye

K

Kamehameha, 27
Kite, 101
Knotweed, 97
Koa, 27

L

Lantana, 24, 25, 26, 27, 30, 31, 96, 98
Large Tiger, 103
Lavender, 20, 31
Leafwings, 102
Legumes, 121, 126, 136
Lepidoptera, 2
Libytheana bachmanii. See American
    Snout
Licorice, 134
Life span, 11, 62
Life stages, 58–61, 91
Light, sufficient, 31, 32, 73, 75, 78, 80
Lilac, 22, 24, 25, 26, 100
Lime, wild, 24
Limenitis. See Viceroy
Limenitis arthemis. See Red-Spotted
    Purple
Little Blues, 17
Live oak, 23
Lobelia, 21, 31
Locust, 134
Long-Tailed Skipper, 10, 22, **136**
Longwing. See Zebra Longwing
Lord Baltimore, 9, **117**
Lorquin's Admiral, 26
Lupine, 17, 20, 27, 128, 129
Lycaena phlaeas. See American Copper
Lycaenidae, 119–124

M

Mailing butterflies, 85
Malachite, 94, **140**
Mallow, 26, 31, 114, 115, 121

Mamake, 27
Marigold, 21, 31
Marjoram, 31
Marketing butterflies, 84
Mating, 56–57, 74, 76–81
Meadow Fritillary, 26, 27, **109**
Meadowsweet, 124
Metalmarks, 16
Metamorphosis, 6
Metric conversion chart, 166
Mexican flame vine, 25
Mexican sunflower, 21, 25
Migration, 3, 10, 149
Milbert's Tortoiseshell, 26
Milkweed, 9, 16, 25, 99, 104
Milkweed butterflies, 103–104. See also
    specific species
Mints, 20, 121
Misting system, 83
Mistletoe, 120
Mock orange, 22
Molting, 46, 74
Monarch, 9, 80, 103, **104,** 105, 149
    caterpillar, 6, 46
    emergence of, 58–59
    host plants, 16, 27, 104
    mating, 76, 80
    migration, 3, 10
    name derivation, 9
    release of, 94
Morning glory, 31
Moths, 11, 12, 149
Mountain sorrel, 122
Mourning Cloak, 24, 26, 60, 92–93, **110**
Moving
    butterflies, 54
    caterpillars, **43**, 51
Mustard, 26, 27
Mustard White, 27, 94
Myths. See Beliefs and lore

N

Name derivations, 9, 92–93
Nasturtium, 21, 24, 27
Native American traditions, 4, 62
Nectar plants, 18, 20–21, 24–27, 73, 83
Neotropicals, 94, 137–140
Net, butterfly, 40–41, 94
Netting for container covers, 73
Nettle, 25, 26, 111, 113
Nettle, false, 113
New Jersey tea, 22
Nicotiana, 31
Nymphalis antiopa. See Mourning Cloak
Nymphalis californica, 93. See also
    Tortoiseshells
Nymphalis vau-album, 93. See also
    Tortoiseshells
Nympholidae (Brush-Footed), 94, 102.
    See also specific species

O

Oak, 23
Orange, 96
    mock, 22
    ornamental, 27
Orange-Barred Sulphur, 94, 125
Orange Sulphur, **128**
Orchid, 97
Oregano, 31
Oregon Swallowtail, 95
Ovipositor, 57

P

Painted Lady, 94, **114–115**
    host plants, 16, 26, 114–115
    life stages, 61
    mating, 57, 77, 80
    migration, 10, 102, 149
Palamedes Swallowtail, 95
Pale Swallowtail, 26
Pansy, 31, 108
Papilio cresphontes. See Giant Swallowtail
Papilio glaucus. See Eastern Tiger
    Swallowtail
Papilionoidea, 10
Papilio polyxenes. See Eastern Black
    Swallowtail
Papilio rutulus, 26, 46. See also Tiger
    Swallowtail
Papilio troilus. See Spicebush
    Swallowtail
Parnassian Swallowtail, 95
Parsley, 21, 24–27, 31, 99
Passionflower, 16, 20, 21, 24, 25, 27,
    108, 137, 139
Patch Butterfly, 25
Pawpaw, 101
Pea, 26, 27, 123
Peach, 143
Pearly Crescentspot, 24, 25, **118**
Pentas, 25, 26, 30, 31, 150
Perennial flowers, 16, 20
Pesticides. See Insecticides
Petroglyphs, 2
Pheromones, 76
Phlox, 20, 24, 25, 26, 99
Phoebis sennae. See Cloudless Sulphur
Phoebus, 27
Photographing butterflies, 151–153
Photoperiod, 75
Phyciodes tharos. See Pearly
    Crescentspot
Pieridae. See Sulphurs; Whites
Pieris rapae. See Cabbage White
Pigmy Blue, 10
Pincushion, 31
Pine White, 94
Pink-Edged Sulphur, 94, 125
Pipevine, 24, 25, 97
Pipevine Swallowtail, 24, 25, 60, **97**, 100

OTHER STOREY TITLES YOU WILL ENJOY

The Backyard Birdhouse Book, by Rene and Christyna M. Laubach. Includes complete plans for eight easy-to-build birdhouses for 25 cavity-nesting species. 216 pages. Paperback. ISBN 1-58017-104-4. Hardcover. ISBN 1-58017-172-9.

The Backyard Bird-Lover's Guide, by Jan Mahnken. Learn about the feeding, territory, courtship, nesting, and parenting behavior of 135 species. 320 pages. Paperback. ISBN 0-88266-927-3.

Grow a Butterfly Garden, by Wendy Potter-Springer. Grow the best species to attract butterflies. 32-page Country Wisdom Bulletin. Paperback. ISBN 0-88266-600-2.

Hand-Feeding Backyard Birds, by Hugh Wiberg. Learn to feed wild birds from your hand with Wiberg's tips on food, weather, time of year, and time of day. 160 pages. Paperback. ISBN 1-58017-181-8.

WoodsWalk, by Henry W. Art and Michael W. Robbins. With enough information on trees, terrain, plants, and wildlife for a hundred walks in the woods, this book is the complete first primer for the inquisitive young naturalist. 128 pages. Paperback. ISBN 1-58017-477-9.

These and other Storey books are available wherever books are sold and directly from Storey Publishing, 210 MASS MoCA Way, North Adams, MA 01247 or by calling 1-800-441-5700. Or visit our Web site at www.storey.com

Metric Conversion Chart

Use the following chart to convert U.S. measurements to metric. Note that the measurements given in this book are approximations, not exact equivalents.

To convert to	When Measurement Given Is	Multiply by
Millimeters	Inches	25
Centimeters	Feet	30
Kilometers	Miles	1.6
Centigrade	Fahrenheit	Subtract 32 from Fahrenheit, multiply by 5, then divide by 9